MOONSHINERS MANUAL

by
Michael Barleycorn

OLIVER PRESS
WILLITS, CALIFORNIA

CHARLES SCRIBNER'S SONS
NEW YORK

Library of Congress Card Number 75-7452
ISBN   0-914400-12-6

ARTIST – DOUG MORAN

First Printing April 1975

OLIVER PRESS
1400 Ryan Creek Road
Willits, California 95490

Distributed by

CHARLES SCRIBNER'S SONS
New York, New York 10012

AUTHOR'S NOTE

The sole intention of this book is to preserve a dying art. An American tradition from 1776 to 1976. A sacred technology of civilized man traced back as far as recorded history. A rapidly fading folklore, waning in the automated, mass-produced world of today.

The art of moonshining has been passed down throughout the centuries by word of mouth and apprenticeship.

This book is the final results of information gathered from scores of men and women across the continent. Saints and sinners alike who made, transported, drank, or busted the infamous moonshine.

The mountains of notes and tapes were organized and carefully researched. The information on them was tried and tested and condensed into a peoples book, "MOONSHINERS MANUAL".

FOR SAM

A special thanks to the many
nameless moonshiners of
North America, and DAVE
HAYES and DON SAMSON,

AND

DICK
DAVE
MIKE
KEITH
KENNY
DENISE
RED RICK AND
THE UNDERGROUND
SHERIFF DEPT.

ARMAND BITEAUX SPIRITUAL ADVISOR

TABLE OF CONTENTS

PREFACE

A moonshiner is a person who makes illegal whiskey. A manual is a how-to-do-it book. The Moonshiners Manual then, tells you how to be a moonshiner.

This book will also acquaint you with the ancient mystique of the art of fermenting and distilling pure organic corn whiskey. It is not intended to encourage the reader to break the law. It is illegal to make any kind of ethanol (drinking alcohol) anywhere in the United States, Canada, or Great Britain. It is estimated that about 200,000 moonshiners are operating in the U. S. alone, depriving the federal government of more than $500 million in tax revenue per year. About one fifth of all hard liquor consumed in this country today is moonshine.

There is a fascinating history of moonshining, blockading, bootlegging and efforts to stamp them out, but you can find books about that history in the library. Encyclopedias will provide the scientific explanation of the chemical processes involved in making alcohol. Temperance pamphlets will warn you of the evils and dangers of booze.

This manual, on the other hand, tells how the moonshiner gets all his stuff together and makes up a batch. You can do it too, if you'll accept the responsibilty for your choice and actions. There's no law against knowing how. THERE IS NO LAW AGAINST HAVING THIS BOOK IN YOUR POSSESSION!

INTRODUCTION

Since the dawn of history men everywhere have discovered ways to make alcoholic beverages. We'll never know quite how these discoveries were made, but it's easy to assume that some food or fruit juice sat around too long, fermented, and got somebody loaded. Primitive man, lofted to a strange new consciousness, was released of fears, and came to think of this beverage—the spirits—as a divine gift. Aristotle knew about distilling, but it was not until the middle ages that hard liquor began to spread.

Times have changed and so has man's understanding of himself and his world around him. Yet distilled alcohol is considered by many as a precious asset, a given right, a downright necessity to soften the harsh edges of living reality. It has always been so.

Cunning men who have sought power over others soon learned that by controlling the people's supply of intoxicating drinks, they consequently gained control over their lives. Governments have taxed liquor throughout the history of civilization to pay for wars. People have been forbidden by their leaders to make their own strong drink in order that the tax coffers might be swelled. Tax collectors have organized veritable armies to enforce prohibition.

But the ordinary man would not be denied his right. He simply went underground or into the back woods to make his squeezin's. Some few have been reduced to feelings of criminal guilt, but a great many men went righteously about the business of building their stills, gathering the necessities, and nursing their hot bubbling pots in secret until they had filled several jugs with the fiery juice that elevated them to new heights of being.

In the early days of the American colonies of England, the King demanded that the colonists drink English booze—or pay dearly for drink from elsewhere. Heavy taxes were placed on American-made liquor. Such action was undeniably one of the chief causes of the Revolutionary War.

Soon after 1776, the Continental Congress imposed high taxes on home-made booze, and prosecuted those who evaded the taxes. Taxes went up in war time, and so did man's need for a strong drink. Whiskey taxes contributed heavily to the financial support of the Revolution, the War of 1812, the Civil War—indeed, it may be seen today how many millions in alcohol taxes are diverted into our military budget.

Is it any wonder then that so many folks, hard pressed for the precious hard earned dollars (more than half the price of a jug) have dared to defy the law?

It's not our place to make any judgment of their morality, nor to make pronouncements about the justness of the law. Ours is merely to explore the activity and product of the likker-lovin' soul who frogs up his own still, sneaks to a hidden location, and attends devotedly to the manufacture of his own supply of fire water.

We are not concerned here with the unscrupulous opportunist who hurriedly produces great quantities of rot gut to sell in the ghettos or the speakeasies for a fast buck. We are looking at the ordinary man who loves an occasional sip of his own potion. He is the moonshiner, the craftsman, alchemist, and wizard. There are countless thousands of his kind in America today who are makin' undercover. A few thousand are caught by the authorities each year and prosecuted by law. The punishment can be ten years, or ten thousand dollars, or maybe they'll just bust up your still and reprimand you. But moonshining goes on.

In this book you will see what the moonshiner is faced with, what he needs, how he goes about his craft, and some of the things he has learned about the distillation of moonshine. It is easy to make good hooch. It is even easier to make deadly poisons.

The process of distilling alcohol from easily available ingredients is amazingly simple. The fine art which is applied to the process is exquisite, demanding,—and rewarding.

Whether or not you decide to try your hand as a moonshiner is entirely up to your own conscience. If it is your choice to learn how, and to proceed to build a still, we ask you to carefully consider the consequences of your decision. We repeat; it is easy to make deadly poison with carelessness or improper equipment. It is possible to get busted by the law. It is exciting to make good sipping whiskey.

Despite the opposition and the merciless laws existing, moonshining continues in kitchens and cellars, creek-beds and backyards everywhere. It is not easy to deny the average man his right to a little nip of his white lightning. He will shine on.

WHISKEY
HOLLOW

PART I

CHAPTER ONE

MOONSHINING IN AMERICA

While most folks reading this book may have at least some familiarity with the history of moonshining in America, it seems appropriate to review that story briefly in these pages. If nothing else, it is an interesting thread in the tapestry of American History. The settling of a new continent called for courage and endurance. It is an accepted fact that alcohol has traditionally aided in the maintenance of both these personal qualities since the dawn of history. Americans are known the world over as a hard-drinking folk, despite the influence of the Puritans and Prohibitionists.

Moonshine has played no small part in the daily lives of countless millions of Americans. Some good, in-depth, definitive books have been written on the subject. If you're interested in such things, you can find them in your library. This chapter will give you a general picture of the background of this craft.

The History Part

Early in the Revolutionary War, the Continental Congress issued about 200 million dollars in paper currency to finance the war. By war's end, that money was worthless. The original new states and the Federal Government were deeply in debt. The colonists were fed up with unfair British

taxes, but the United States, needing funds with which to operate and to pay their debts, levied new taxes on property and goods. In 1791 a tax was levied on the making of whiskey. This aroused the anger of farmers in remote areas, because it was easier to convert their corn and rye crops into whiskey than to transport the bulky grains to distant markets on poor roads. The fact was, a jug of whiskey actually had more spending value than paper money.

The new law gave permission to government agents to enter the homes of small whiskey producers and to collect taxes from them. This brought about a general protest all over the country. Congress soon lifted the tax for the smallest whiskey makers in such states as Virginia and North Carolina; but many moonshiners where the tax remained, especially in western Pennsylvania, still refused to pay the tax. To put teeth in the enforcement of the whiskey tax, the Federal Government sent marshals in to arrest the rebel ringleaders. That was in 1794. The marshals were met by angry mobs of farmers. In several locations, bitter fights broke out. Many people were killed and wounded.

In a move to squash the Whiskey Rebellion, and to reestablish respect for the Federal Government, President George Washington ordered troops to Pennsylvania. After a long confrontation with thousands of rebellious citizens, involving shoot-outs and house-burnings, the troops restored order. They arrested several of the leaders near Philadelphia. Two of these leaders were found guilty of treason, but both were later pardoned by Washington.

And so, in the Whiskey Rebellion of 1794, the people of an infant nation learned that the Federal Government did indeed have the power to enforce its laws with the individual states. That single action cost the government about 1½ million dollars. An interesting sidelight to George Washington's action in this matter is that a whiskey still is known to have been in operation at his home in Mt. Vernon about that time.

That military action didn't ring the death knell to moonshining, however. Far from it. The early Americans loved their strong "likker" and preferred the hearty corn squeezin's to the watered and flavored stuff coming from licensed distilleries. The government had authorized certain distillers to produce legal whiskey for commercial consumption. Federal agents were on tap to monitor quality and, of course, to collect seven cents for Uncle Sam on every gallon produced. But the hardy new Americans from Ireland and Scotland, who had developed the art of distilling in the northern part of the British Isles, were not easily discouraged. Along with French and German distillers, thousands continued to defy the tax laws by moving their stills from the farmyards into the boondocks, where the tax collectors would not find them so easily. They smuggled their goods into the marketplace in blockade wagons, covering their jugs and barrels with corn stalks or hay.

The federal tax agents persisted in seeking out the illicit whiskey makers, forcing them deeper into the back woods. Still raids and the arrests and convictions of moonshiners instigated a mass movement of farmers from the northern Appalachian Mountains southward into the remote regions of the Smokies and the Blue Ridge Mountains of Virginia, North Carolina, Kentucky, Tennessee and Georgia. No doubt, moonshiners have operated in all of the states, but the southern Appalachian Mountains have long been known as the heart of moonshine country ever since. Here, in the remote valleys, far from cities and main roads, the rugged mountain folk pursued the makin' of stump whiskey in relative peace for more than a century. Not that the federal tax collectors did not continue to seek out their stills and to ambush their blockade wagons as they shipped their makin's into the growing population centers of the South. The government continued to punish those who defied the law and refused to pay the taxes. Penalties for convicted offenders were severe. Long prison terms and steep fines were designed to discourage others from risking the manufacture of illegal whiskey.

But as a general rule, most of the people in the mountain communities were sympathetic with the moonshiners, and they often conspired to foil the tax agents in their work. Even local judges, trying the offenders, often suspended sentences, or even found their arrested neighbors not guilty of violating the law. Reports by tax officers to their superiors in Washington indicated great difficulty in enforcing the law. Feelings ran so high among the moonshiner's faction that tax agents were often tarred and feathered, or even murdered for trying to interfere with the makin' and selling of their precious mountain spirits. Tax agents who shot moonshiners were quickly sentenced to hang on charges of murder, while moonshiners who killed lawmen were often freed on grounds of self-defense.

In the year 1800, however, Thomas Jefferson was elected President. One of his early moves was to do away with the "infernal" tax on whiskey. He regarded it as an infringement of freedom. For more than half a century afterwards —except for three years during the War of 1812—whiskey makers were free to ply their trade or hobby without interruption. It was to be the one period in American history without conflict about the legality of moonshine. The roads and rivers of the expanding young nation were teeming with wagons and barges carrying home-made likker to the thirsty communities and isolated frontiers. Special makin's like Kentucky Bourbon, Monongahela Rye and Tennessee Sippin' Whiskey were famous and prized wherever drinking folk met.

By 1850, a strong prohibitionist movement began to make itself felt, particulaily in the major cities of the East. Heavy pressures were being exerted by individual groups to stamp out all manufacture and consumption of fermented and distilled spirits. During this time, of course, the seeds of the Civil War were taking root in the industrial Northern states and the predominantly agricultural states of the South. When the war broke out in 1860, the government focused little attention on the moonshine problem. In 1862,

Lincoln appointed a Commissioner of Internal Revenue to supervise the collection of income taxes and increased excise taxes on alcoholic beverages. At that time, the U. S. was demanding two dollars a gallon on all hard liquor. Moonshining thrived during the Civil War. As the war dragged on, the beleaguered South was desperately in need of grains to feed the people and their army; consequently, there was much criticism of the wasting of good corn and rye for the making of moonshine. The law of supply and demand prevailed, and the drinking folks got their drink.

In the years following the Civil War, the quantity of moonshine produced throughout the country increased significantly. Once again the government, with its vigorous new Internal Revenue outfit, sent forays of tax collectors into the mountains and cities to ferret out the whiskey makers. When Ulysses S. Grant was elected to the Presidency in 1868, he backed the tax office with funds and military support to establish, once and for all, the government's intentions to control the moonshine people. Colonel George Custer, after his time as a Civil War officer and before his stint at Little Big Horn, was sent to Kentucky to fight moonshiners.

New laws were brought into effect—not by popular vote, but by federal mandate—to punish all manner of violators. In effect, during the 1870's, a state of near-war existed between the "revenooers" and the moonshiners. Three to four thousand stills were seized yearly. Six to eight thousand persons were arrested and convicted every year. Scores of "revenooers" and moonshiners were killed and injured. The '70's saw the most intense conflict so far between the U. S. Government and those who would not be denied their right to make and drink a little sippin' whiskey. It would not be until the Prohibition years that the battle would rage so intensely again.

It should be borne in mind that, even though many commercial distilleries had been licensed to make and sell legal liquor, a large portion of the country's expanding population was still buying and drinking home-made rum, brandy and whiskey.

Simultaneously with this deep concern over the matter of people's rights regarding drinking, Carrie Nation and her axewielding accomplices were establishing the Women's Christian Temperance Union. Thousands of Americans, principally women, who had felt the effects of alcoholism on their loved ones, joined together to demand an end to the manufacture and consumption of **all** alcoholic beverages. It can be seen that, in those years, a great deal of emotional and physical energy was being expended by both factions over the matter of the good and evil nature of drinking spirits.

For many Americans, these were hard times. Working conditions in the sweat shops of this expanding industrial nation were often grim and exhausting. An increasing number of people turned to alcohol for solace and escape. The Demon Rum became a literal enemy to those whose lives were adversely affected by the hard drinkers.

During this era, while the Federal Government was imposing its power to collect whiskey taxes and to end illicit moonshining, a great scandal was brewing which was to be known as the Whiskey Ring. It seems that during U. S. Grant's administration as President, a conspiracy of licensed whiskey manufacturers and government officials grew to rather enormous proportions. These distillers (mostly in St. Louis) and members of federal agencies were pocketing large sums of cash that were intended to go to the tax coffers. In 1875 investigators fingered the offenders and put a stop to the cheating. Some of the conspirators held high positions in the IRS and the Treasury Department, a fact which left a blot on Grant's entire administration. Grant himself, by the way, had a pretty good reputation as a lover of hard likker.

15

Despite the concentrated efforts of tax collectors, federal marshals, temperance leaders and prohibitionists, thousands of folks all over the nation continued to set up their stills and run their squeezin's. The love of an occasional nip of mountain dew was too strong to be intimidated by armed revenooers or by new laws. The moonshiners were here to stay. It seems that for every still seized, another would spring up somewhere else. For every convicted violater who went to the hoosegow, another began distilling.

As a result of the opposition to the demon drink, many individual states voted to prohibit the sale and use of alcoholic beverages. The natural reaction, since the drinker **would** have his drink, was usually an increase in moonshining activity in the dry states to make up for the loss of legal spirits. Needless to say, this led to an increase in "crime." The Internal Revenue people seldom relaxed in their efforts to punish the wrongdoers and to collect what they considered their rightful taxes.

It can be seen that moonshining has been an underground activity much of the time since the founding of the United States government; indeed, since even before that, inasmuch as the British had long attempted to discourage the consumption of anything other than British-made liquor. And so moonshining has continued through history to be an activity purely in defiance of the government's right to say us nay.

Just prior to the outbreak of World War I, several serious attempts were made by prohibitionists and Congress to enact national laws that would make it illegal to manufacture, sell, buy or drink any form of alcohol. These efforts were postponed by the nation's involvement in the war in Europe, but in 1917, legislation was undertaken to make the country "dry." The Webb-Kenyon Law went into effect in 1920, creating one of the most drastic scenes the populace had ever played, with regard to alcoholic beverages. From that time on, it was a crime to have anything to do with beer, wine or liquor. Law enforcement agencies at every level focused great energies on enforcing the Prohibition Law. The demand for moonshine was incredible. Throughout the nation, stills were set up in every kind of hidden place to satisfy the demand for drink. As the demand increased, the product was made with greater haste and carelessness. Even many traditional moonshine craftsmen, greedy for the money to be made, resorted to cranking out low-quality alcohol which had not been properly purified. Fusel oils, zinc salts and blue vitriols (all undesirable by-products of careless distilling) were often left in the product, which caused a variety of tragic effects upon those who were unfortunate enough to drink the stuff. Nerve damage, blindness, paralysis, insanity and death became not uncommon among the imbibers of this cheap underground rotgut or popskull whiskey.

These were the days when big money could be made by making and selling anything that would pass for liquor. Secret taverns, called "speakeasies," sprang up all over the country, where ordinary folks who knew the password could buy a few drinks. Most of them didn't last long, because once the word was out, it wasn't long before the local cops were there to raid the place and load all its customers in the "Black Maria" for a trip to the clink. By the same token, it was also not long before another speakeasy appeared in the neighborhood, perhaps disguised as a sandwich shop. The people **would** have their booze, and many were willing to risk jail or fines to have it. Pocket flasks and garter flasks became fashionable to carry.

With all the money to be made supplying the drinking population with their only source of alcohol, it was not long before big syndicates were formed, led by tough gangster bosses who were willing to kill indiscriminately to protect their networks of moonshiners, bootleggers and speakeasy operators. These were the days of the hoods and mobsters like Al Capone and Dutch Schultz, men who amassed fortunes and personal power by their anti-prohibition activities.

Enter the Mafia. Conditions were perfect for dedicated opportunists. Widespread, no-nonsense organizations were set up which involved suppliers, truckers, makers, warehouses, importers, exporters, dealers and all manner of henchmen. Skilled moonshiners and engineers were recruited to develop giant stills capable of running thousands of gallons per day. Truckloads of grains were purchased in bulk directly from the farms. Sugar and other ingredients were bought by the carload. Large bakeries were taken over to provide yeast. Souped-up cars were especially engineered and modified so that adventurous young men could transport the green hooch, hot off the still, into the marketplace. These were the "trippers" who dodged and raced the squad cars of pursuing lawmen over rough mountain roads and crowded city streets. Big money was made by anybody who felt gutsy enough and clever enough to avoid arrest. Bunglers and squealers were done away with.

The Mafia became the biggest, most successful and most feared of all the big syndicates, amassing untold millions with its secret powerful operation. The number of arrests, still seizures, beatings and killings that took place during this "great experiment" far exceeded the bloody years of the 1870's. The effects of the Prohibition Law still remain a sordid memory in United States history.

For thirteen long years America was legally dry and wildly wet. During those years the government was literally at war with moonshiners and bootleggers. Finally, a nation weary of conflict, subterfuge, hypocrisy and low-grade hooch, voted in 1933 to repeal the law. Some states chose to remain dry by local option, but licensed commercial distilleries were back in operation again, and moonshiners went back to small-scale production. Moonshining was still illegal.

By 1941, the feds were seizing twelve thousand stills a year. When the U. S. declared war, the excise tax on liquor was boosted to six dollars a gallon. More and more states and counties voted "dry." Both of these factors seemed to stimulate moonshine activity—and, of course, federal attempts to stop it. During those times, sugar, metals and gasoline were hard to get, forcing makers and bootleggers to be even more creative in finding new ways to supply the national need—a need made stronger by the closing down of most commercial distilleries during the war years. With all the tension and hardship of war, the people wanted their "escape juice." Black market booze intensified the war on illegal makers to a new high. The Mafia continued to dominate the underground industry until the sugar shortage forced them to seek their principal income in other ways, namely in the growing market for heroin and opium. But that's another story.

The '50's and '60's saw a gradual decline in the drama of illicit liquor. They were days of relative peace and affluence for most folks not involved in the two wars in Asia. The demand for moonshine decreased. Fewer people were directly involved in the battle with the revenooers. A goodly amount of moonshining took place, but on a smaller and quieter scale.

Today, American drinkers spend nearly five billion dollars a year for legal liquor. Alcohol taxes, currently $10.50 per gallon, account for about five percent of the country's internal revenue. While moonshining is today only a shadow of its previous character, there remain thousands of stills in operation from coast to coast. The IRS continues to maintain a staff of men to investigate and curtail the makers, and they are aided by state, county and local law enforcement agencies. Even in the southern Appalachians, where moonshining had its fullest and most romantic flowering, the old-timers lament that moonshinin' ain't what it used to be.

Today, as increasing numbers of people throughout the nation are moving away from the cities to find peace and self-sufficiency in the country, stills are springing up again.

In the back-to-the-land movement, however, the emphasis is not on money-making. It is rather—as in bygone days—a means of providing a little sippin' likker for family and friends, at a price the poor man can afford.

We are experiencing a reappearance of the attitude that the government may have overstepped its rights in denying the people a little drink of home-made. It is, after all, claim the rebels, a victimless crime—if indeed it **is** a crime. The few cents or dollars that would have gone for taxes, say the modern day moonshiners, would hardly cover the cost of its collection.

Is moonshining really coming back? Has it ever been away? Is the government going to launch a new attack on the makers of illicit spirits? Or will popular vote finally change an archaic law of questionable constitutionality, and bring a new freedom to enjoy an occasional sip of home-made squeezin's?

Only history will tell.

CHAPTER TWO

INTRODUCTION TO MOONSHINING
Principles of Distillation

To **distill** is to separate one liquid from another of a different boiling point or evaporation temperature. Such is the case with alcohol and water, or fermented mash and whiskey. Alcohol (ethanol) will vaporize at 172.8 degrees F. (or 173 degrees F. as we shall call it from here on.) Water vaporizes at 212 degrees F. Therefore, if the mixture were heated to 173 degrees, the alcohol would vaporize and leave the water behind.

The next step is to capture the alcoholic vapors, move them away from the rest of the mash and cool them enough to cause them to condense or liquify, so that they may be bottled and/or disposed of properly.

There are two basic steps involved in getting from cracked corn to mountain dew. First, the corn has to be **fermented.** What happens here is that you add sugar to the corn, add water, and then yeast. This mess is called **mash.** The yeast will multiply in the warm water and will exist on the sugar, which it eats. As the yeast consumes the sugar, it excretes carbon dioxide and ethanol or alcohol (more commonly known as loose juice.) The alcohol stays with the mash, and the carbon dioxide bubbles off into the air. The yeast will multiply and consume, and produce the magic juice with enthusiasm. But as all good things must come to an end, and this is no exception, the yeast produces so much alcohol that it starts killing itself faster than it can multiply and the process grinds to a halt as the sugar is used up and the yeast dies off. The liquid you have left is a crude beer containing approximately 16% alcohol: the mash.

The second step is to distill this fermented mash. Quite simply, you put the mash in a sealed pot and heat it to 173 degrees. The vapors, as they rise out of the pot, move into a copper tube which conducts the steam to the condenser barrel. Here the tube enters the condenser and coils around and around inside the barrel, which is filled with constantly circulating cold water, and emerges through the wall of the barrel at the bottom. As the vapors cool, they condense into a liquid state again, and the drops can be joyously collected in your jug.

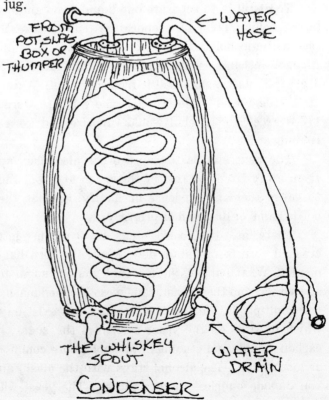

FROM POT, SLAG BOX OR THUMPER

← WATER HOSE

THE WHISKEY SPOUT

WATER DRAIN

CONDENSER

If you want to try a simple demonstration of the basic process in your kitchen, here's a little trick you can do in a few minutes:

Pour about a pint or so of any pure wine (not the cheaper synthetic commercial brands) into a stainless steel or copper sauce-pan. Put a cup or small bowl in the middle of the pan so that the cup is in the wine, but the wine is not in the cup. Now, get a plate, saucer, or bowl that will cover the pan as a lid. This lid should have a curving or rounded bottom so it can be filled with cold water and ice cubes, so when the wine is heated and the spirit vapors rise to the cold lid, they will condense and drip into the cup below.

Bring the temperature up very slowly over a medium-low heat. As it approaches 173 degrees the drops of crude brandy will begin to fill your cup. When you have enough to taste and examine, STOP! Do not continue heating for more than about five minutes.

This method is not by any means suggested as a substitute for a still. There is no control over temperature, proof, or quality. Simply a demonstration of the basics and a taste of things to come.

In a nut shell, that's how you make scorpion juice. But hold on a minute, there. You ain't a moonshiner yet. There's a lot of other stuff you got to know before you're ready to start. Read on. The thing is, while it is all very simple to vaporize and condense alcohol, it's also very painstaking work with a whole lot of critical do's and don'ts. So pay close attention.

What Moonshine is Like

Have you ever tasted real, honest-to-goodness moonshine? If you have, then you know it's like no beverage you can buy in the store. First off, pure corn liquor, before it's aged or adulterated, is crystal clear, like spring water. The fumes will make your eyeballs smart and they'll pucker your nostrils before you can get a fruit jar full up to your lips. The first taste is deceptive. It can seem harmless enough to the tongue, but it goes down your tubes like a highly seasoned swig of napalm, instantly sounding battle stations to your entire nervous system. It also will creep up on you. As one codger told us, "it's a good idea to be settin' on the ground when you drink it, so you won't have so far to fall."

It's no joke, gentle reader, one jigger of gen-yoo-wine panther juice will knock your socks off, simultaneously jolting you out of the sober state. A loose high? You bet your best pair of overalls it is. If you're new to mountain dew, you'd best go real easy at first, cause, lord love ya', a couple of snorts can get you rapidly shitfaced, falling-down drunk in no time flat.

Ignorant folks have been known to chug-a-lug a mere pint of the fiery stuff and drop very suddenly dead on the floor. It ain't called **sippin'** whiskey for nothing. Please understand that in no way is the foregoing word of caution designed to alarm or discourage. The point is, **any** alcohol when drunk too fast can overwhelm your body. It's just that the alcohol content of moonshine can be pretty high. Drink it easy. Treat it with respect. Have a nice time. One comes to have a profound regard for authentic creepin' whiskey. Are you getting the picture? Do you begin to see why, as one whiskey guru told us, "moonshinin' gits in your blood!"

The Moonshine Mystique

The information given in the Moonshiners Manual came down to us through a long line of folks who have, amongst 'em squeezed out many thousands of gallons of ruckus juice in their time. We'll pass along as much of what the moonshiner needs to know as we can. Along with that, there's this "mystique" we keep talking about. Moonshining is intriguing, partly because it's illegal and partly because it **can** be dangerous if you don't mind your P's and Q's. It's intriguing, too, because you're makin' your own traditional, high-powered moonshine from scratch. No doubt about it, makin' is fun and drinkin' is funner. There are those living among us for whom the fine art has become the ultimate adventure. Let's see if we can pick up a taste of that adventure.

The moonshiner and his partners pick the location for their whiskey makin' operation with care. They may scout the backwoods for several days before finding a spot suitable for all the conditions of moonshining. First off, of course, they want to be far enough from the roads and houses to avoid detection. If they are going to have a wood fire under the still pot, there's the smoke to think about. They wouldn't want an alert forestry lookout to dispatch a crew of firefighters to the area.

Despite its isolation, the still site has to be fairly accessible. The moonshiner has to carry in barrels, still, sacks of corn and sugar, jugs, hoses, and other gear—and carry it out again, undetected. He usually unloads all his stuff near the road and drives his truck away so it won't stand as a signal of suspicious activity to passers-by. It's not uncommon for such passers-by to encounter men with squirrel rifles along the road who tell the strangers they'd best turn back, "'cause there ain't nothin' of interest in these parts." The moonshiner might carry his supplies and equipment down into a wooded ravine. To avoid creating obvious paths through the woods, he often takes several different routes to and from the still site.

A major consideration for a still site is the availability of an unlimited water supply. A creek, ideally with a bit of a waterfall, can provide the cold water required for the operation. A downhill slope from the still can carry off the excess water flow, so there won't be too much mud to wade around in. Often this excess water from the condenser can be diverted back into the stream, but the veteran moonshiner takes care that someone downstream doesn't detect the presence of the waste products of the operation. Many a revenooer caught his man by means of such clues.

As you can see, there's a lot of stuff to carry in and out of the woods for a whiskey run. Two or three men are usually required to carry it off. Too many people involved, though, are apt to arouse the curiosity of the neighboring community, which is, of course, always a bad idea.

In the old days, moonshiners sometimes liked to set up their stills in caves, or if they lived way off in the sticks, they would build fairly permanent still houses to shelter themselves and their equipment, thus simplifying many aspects of the operation. But if the local revenooer was on the prowl in the area, the still house was a dead giveaway.

It's not uncommon for the moonshiner to pack in grub and bedrolls for a stay of several days at the site while fermenting and distilling several barrels of mash. This often means lanterns and night fires, both of which contribute to the possibility of getting caught, or he works by the light of the full moon, which he always loves, and which enhances the run in many subtle and wonderful ways. That is, of course, where he got his name.

A little paranoia is not an uncommon state of mind for the working moonshiner—although his sense of his own inalienable right to make himself a little whiskey, and his constitutionally guaranteed right to the pursuit of happiness, usually see him through.

Once the mash is started in its barrel, the die is cast. Nothing short of an officer of the law can persuade the true moonshiner to abandon his post. Through heat and rain, cold and darkness, he remains attentively by his precious cauldrons and tends them with care until his work is done.

At any moment there is the outside possibility of the sudden emergence from the woods of an armed revenooer, demanding his arrest and surrender. Some will run into the woods, leading the persecutor on a merry chase through glen and glade. Others will submit to handcuffs or agree to appear before the local law at a given time the next day. The stills are slugged with axes. The whiskey is poured out on the ground. Mash barrels are overturned and smashed. A sordid prospect indeed, yet one which every moonshiner knows is a real possibility.

But the bust is still a relatively infrequent event. Witness the fact that every fifth drink of hard liquor consumed in the United States today is moonshine!

On a successful run, when the mash is played out, and the white mule is safely in the jugs, the moonshiners then pack all their barrels, pots, jugs and miscellaneous stuff back through the woods to be picked up by the truck, or hide the equipment and leave no traces of the run—if they are still able to walk after sampling their product.

There is cleaning up to do, scrubbing of barrels and pots, securing the fire, picking up old sacks, and any other evidence of activity there. This would obviously be the hardest part to get into after sampling, but the smart moonshiner takes no chances of spoiling a good location for a future run. In some areas where revenooers abound, the 'shiner is forced to keep finding new locations to avoid detection. The fact is, the experienced moonshiner learns a lot of clever tricks, not only in the makin' of good hooch but in avoiding the law. Revenooers and moonshiners develop a great respect for each other's cleverness. It's the ancient love story that evolves between the hunter and his prey.

You've just had a little peek at the adventure of a country run, as though you had looked down from the top of a ravine at the moonshiners below. In the remainder of this book, we'll take you through the underbrush to the bottom of the ravine, where you will learn the do's and dont's of making your own spirits. Your location may be different. It may be in your back yard, your attic, cellar or garage, or maybe you'll choose the simplified, civilized method of makin' in your kitchen which we'll describe later. But wherever and however the makin' takes place, may it always carry some of that old country backwoods moonshine mystique.

PART II

CHAPTER THREE

THE COUNTRY STILL

The traditional country still has been made in a thousand shapes and sizes since ancient times. The design suggested here is taken from a typical home-made country still —one that's turned out a whole lot of really fine corn likker. We'll tell you how to build one like it, and we'll add a few suggestions for simplifying or modifying it according to your ingenuity, needs, and the availability of materials.

Building your own country still from scratch could cost from one to two hundred dollars or more, depending on the size and particulars of the still you choose to build. If you're into supplying a little whiskey for your family and neighbors over a period of time, that's not a bad investment at all. Besides your still will pay for itself in a very short time in saved taxes.

No doubt about it, it **is** going to take some time, effort, and money. As we've heard many a time when inquiring about the craft, "ain't no lazy man gonna make wheesky." But if you figure you've got as much brains as the old codger in the woods who built this "typical" still, then head on. Just follow instructions, use your head, and keep in mind the basic principles, and you really have all the room in the world to vary from the basic plan.

If on the other hand, building a country still seems too much to tackle, or if you live on the 14th floor on the corner of Second and Main where one wouldn't be of much use to you, take heart. Read this chapter for the basics. Later we'll show you a much simpler method and equipment you can set up, with easily available materials, in your own kitchen.

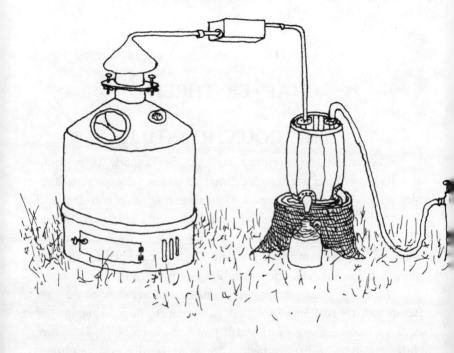

The typical country still illustrated here will serve as a model and will be covered in detail. Any variations in the size and capacity, according to your wants or needs, should be made proportionately throughout the construction. You can make your still larger or smaller, as you please, as long as you understand the important relationships involved. There are many aspects to consider.

This still is designed to get from one to three gallons of good, hot whiskey from one barrel (50 gallons) of mash. That's enough to supply the farm or ranch and a few neighbors for a while without having to run the still too often. A little white lightning goes a long way.

The main components of the still are: the kettle or pot, the cap, the slag-box, the thumper (if one is used), condenser, and a heating system. You'll also be working with jugs and barrels and such but these things are not considered as parts of the still itself. We will take up each of the components separately, explaining its design and function, and show how they work together. With a basic design and knowledge of the functional requirements of these parts, you should be able to come up with a still that will fit your needs and that can be constructed from materials available to you.

This still is made completely out of copper. All stills should be made only out of copper or stainless-steel, or a combination of the two. No other metals should be used. Any other metals in contact with the whiskey during a run, will react adversely, producing toxins, some deadly, which will contaminate the run.

It has a 35 gallon **total** capacity and a 25 gallon mash capacity. This means it will run 25 gallons of mash at a time, leaving 10 gallons of space between the mash level and the cap. This space accomodates the bubbling head as the mash is cooked and prevents it from "puking" into the cap and "clouding" your run. This is an ideal size for the average small time maker. It will run one-half of the standard 55 gallon mash (or wine) barrel at a time. The size of your still should compliment the size of your mash barrel and vice versa, so that the still will handle the volume of mash your mash barrel can produce. This one requires two full runs per barrel. A pot of twice the capacity obviously will distill one full barrel per run.

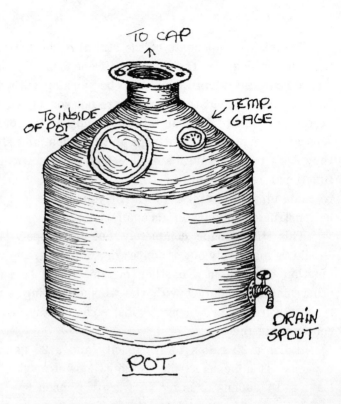

TO CAP

TO INSIDE OF POT

TEMP. GAGE

DRAIN SPOUT

POT

The Pot

Here is where the fermented mash is heated to the magic temperature of 173 which, in turn releases the elixir as a vapor, sending it on its merry way. The pot may be your toughest acquisition but it's the heart of your still and should be put together with loving care. As stated before, it is made only of copper or stainless-steel. All joints and seams should be **silver soldered only** on copper pots and heli-arc welded on stainless steel.

If you're really lucky you might be able to find an old copper milk can or laundry boiler of some sort that can be converted into a still pot. Maybe you'll find a big old stainless steel pressure cooker or soup pot in a restaurant supply or surplus outfit. Persevere. Poke around. Ask people, discreetly. Some folks may even suspect you want the copper, or what have you, for a still, of all things. Ridiculous. Although some folks may be unsympathetic to the devil's brew and/or its manufacture, there's no harm done in asking around. You can't always get what you want, but with a little perseverance, you can get what you need.

If you are going to build the pot out of sheet copper, remember that it's going to be pressurized and all seams should be solid and air-tight. If you've worked with sheet copper before then you'll know how easily it crimps and kinks when bent. If not, then go easy. You might try forming the necessary curves by bending it gently and gradually around a large tree trunk or post.

If cutting, bending, and soldering copper seems a bit out of your line then you might try to find a metalworker, or equally competent friend, who will frog it up for you, for some cash on delivery, or promise of a share of the booty. Almost everybody appreciates a little nip now and then and might be obliged to assist in return for a private stash of your brew.

However it is built, it should have an inlet near the top so you have access to the inside for filling the still and doubling while the still is assembled and the cap is in place, during the run. This opening should be a good five inches or so in diameter to allow for easy filling from a bucket and to admit your arm for cleaning purposes before and after the run. This hole must also seal up pressure-tight, but the cap must be fairly easy to remove and replace during the run when it is hot.

At the very top of the pot is the neck and a lip which the cap will connect to. The cap has a sort of collared sleeve which fits inside the neck and seats on the lip of the pot.

Next, very important, but not quite essential in a pinch, is the temperature gauge. Not quite essential because the experienced moonshiner can learn to tell the temperature by his senses and the little telltale signs which say that "all is well", or "cut back the flame, it's getting too hot!" But until you've mastered these arts you had best use a temperature gauge. It should read at least between 100 degrees and 200 degrees, and be mounted in an easy-to-read location near the top of the pot with the heat sensor in the center of the cooking mash. This will give you the most accurate reading.

The pot must have a drain at the bottom to empty the played-out mash at the end of each run. A one-inch, faucet-type valve will allow you to empty the still at a good rate.

Finally, you'll find that a couple of handles, high on either side, will make for easy transporting.

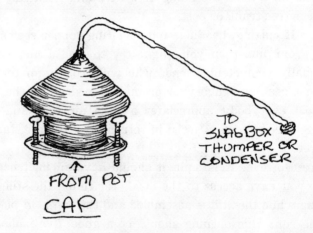

TO
SLAB BOX
THUMPER OR
CONDENSER

↑
FROM POT
CAP

The Cap

The cap, as shown in the sketch, is a cone-shaped unit that serves as sort of an expansion chamber as it also funnels the steam into the connecting tube. It should be easy to clean. The neck of the cap fits snugly into the neck of the pot. A gasket of cardboard, rubber, or flour and water is placed between the lips which are then clamped tight with mini C-clamps or some sort of wing-bolt arrangement. This connection can be semi-permanent, as you won't need to break the seal once the run has started, but should be removable for cleaning and easy transportation.

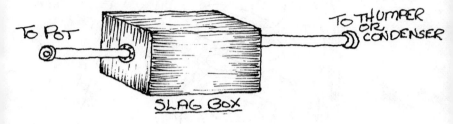

TO POT

TO THUMPER OR CONDENSER

SLAG BOX

The Slag Box

Another one of those optional but highly recommended accessories to a good still is the slag box. A simple purifying device, it is a copper or wooden expansion chamber which allows the vapors to spread out, causing the heavier impurities to settle to the bottom as the lighter, purest alcohol rises to the top and into the conducting tube again, on the way to becoming whiskey.

As the impurities like fusel oils (a toxic by-product of the process) collect and condense at the bottom of the slag box, you would need a little petcock at the bottom for occasional draining of the nasty stuff.

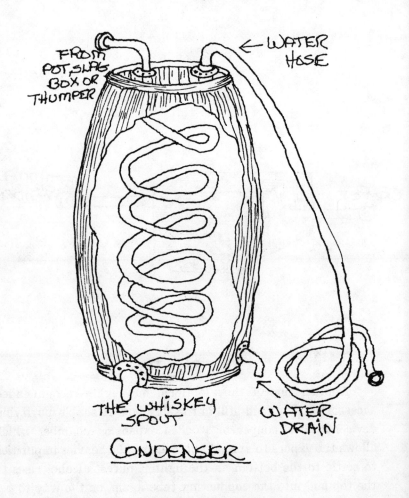

From pot, slag box or thumper

← Water hose

The whiskey spout

Water drain

CONDENSER

The Condenser

And here is where the steam is finally returned to a liquid state and is dispensed into your waiting jug. The vapors enter the flake box (condenser) inside the copper tubing and begin spiraling downward in a coil. The flake box is filled with constantly circulating cold water. There should be at least 10 feet of tubing in the box to give the vapors a complete chance to cool. Quarter-inch to three-eighths diameter copper tubing will be sufficient here, and about a foot of it extends out of the bottom of the barrel.

A valuable tip: Before you start bending the tube into coils you should fill it with sand or sawdust to avoid crimping. You can again use a tree or pole to shape the coils. Don't forget to rinse the sand and sawdust from the tube with a hose. The coil must be secured at the top as it enters the condenser, and there must be a drain hole at the bottom which can be adjusted to equalize the amount of water flowing in and flowing out.

What some of the boys used to do, was mount the flake box off to the side and below a creekbed and run the cold water down a conduit or hollowed sapling or hose into the top of the barrel. Some folks just let it fill and overflow. Others feel it is better to poke a hole or two at the bottom to let the excess water escape. A faucet-type valve, again, is the best.

You might want to do some trenching around the condenser, as several hours of spilling water would probably make a mud puddle tit-high to a ten foot injun.

One little tidbit regarding the condenser. You'll want a pretty good seal around the end of the "worm" or tube as it extends through the bottom of the barrel. Otherwise, water will leak out and run down the tube, and into your pure corn squeezin's. You wouldn't want that, now would you?

A quick note about car radiators. There have been thousands of cases in the history of moonshining in which adequate materials for making a good still have simply not been available. You've no doubt heard that car radiators, for example, have been occasionally used as condensers. Well friend, we have only one comment about radiators. That is FORGET THEM!!! There is no way to be sure that they are clean inside, not to mention the fact that all joints and seams are held together by lead solder. Bad news. Just leave car radiators alone, even new ones. Please!

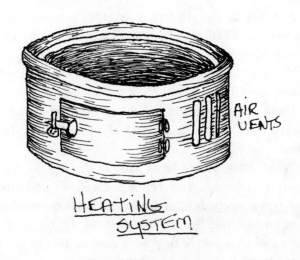

AIR VENTS

HEATING SYSTEM

Heating System

It seems unlikely that any self-respecting moonshiner ever used the term "heating system," but since there are several ways to apply heat to your kettle, we'll use that term now. What it will need to do is heat the mash to 173 degrees and hold it there for many hours. Kitchen stoves are nice, in the kitchen. A propane or gas burner could prove perfect for you. The honest-to-gosh backwoods maker built a fire under his pot and tended it carefully with a large supply of hardwood cut to various sizes, ready to feed into the fire.

The illustrated heating system works very nicely and is simple to get together. It's the top third of a 55-gallon steel oil drum. A hole was cut in the top, just a little smaller than the base of the still it is to support.

This exposes the bottom of the still to direct flame from the fire box while providing a lip to support the considerable weight (over 200 pounds) of the still, filled with mash. A hinged door cut out of the front can adjust the air flow with the help of a rear vent, ideally with a chimney or smokestack.

If you're going to invent your own firebox, remember the weight that must be supported. Design it to use the heat efficiently. A great many of the backwood hillbillies built stone firepits with great chimneys enclosing the entire still pot, using all the heat of a minimal flame. With practice or experience (really the same thing) and one of these giant stone heaters that draws the heat and smoke around the sides of the kettle, you can control the temperature of the mash to ½ of a degree anywhere you want it. It should be apparent here that the main factor to consider about the heating system is precise temperature control and efficient heat use.

The experienced moonshiner developed a fine art in tending his hardwood firepit. You may understandably prefer to use a simple propane burner, or maybe you'll rig one up from an old cafe grill. If you do consider gas, please keep the gas tank at least 10 feet from your flame.

Another thing to add to your list of supplies is something to catch the squeezins' in. Some of the old timers used to catch their likker in an oaken tub or bucket. But mud, oak

leaves, inebriated insects, and the like are sometimes disheartening floating around in the beautiful crystal elixir. The ideal catchin' jug is one of those clear glass, five gallon, commerical water bottles. (You know Sparklets, or Culligan, spring or artesian water merchants). Not actually one of the still parts, but most essential, wouldn't you agree?

So, there you have your still. Lord knows it ain't Jack Daniels' distillery, but it can brew up the finest moonshine this side of Istanbul, if you take your time, do it right, and have your equipment properly constructed and clean. Just stick to the principles. Every still, funky or slick, has its own unique character.

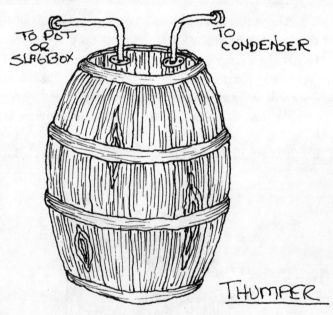

TO POT OR SLAGBOX

TO CONDENSER

THUMPER

The Thumper Barrel

This thumper is an option not suggested for the rookie. The advanced moonshiner, though, might take note of this purifying device as an addition to his basic still. It goes in between the slag box and the condenser and can be considered as an elaborate slag box, only instead of an empty box, the thumper is an air-tight oak barrel filled with fermenting mash. The steam enters at the bottom of the barrel, having to make it's way to the top as it bubbles up. Again the lighter purest alcohol will rise to the top and continue via a connecting tube on to the condenser. The heavier impurities are trapped in the thumper and remain behind in the mash. When the run is finished, the "thumped mash" is put into the still to be run off, and the thumper is filled with fresh mash. The name thumper came from the deep rhythmic sound made as the bubbles forced their way through the mash in the barrel.

Actually, unless you're planning on doing high volume, multiple runs and rotating many barrels over an extended period of time, then you're not quite ready for the thumper. But at least you're learning how to talk moonshine.

CHAPTER FOUR

THE MASH
Corn Liquor

There are many ways to make the mash. Every moonshiner has a different story, and often it happens that two stories contradict each other on more than one point. There are no academies or degrees in moonshining, and each man is his own school of thought. Of all the grains and fruits from which whiskey or brandy is made, each has its own unique contribution to the taste and texture of the hooch. How you blend the ingredients is largely a matter of taste. As in any art though, and in the art of moonshining, there are basics. Try a tested trusted recipe first. It has been used many times and it works. After we have been through the basic story we'll take up some possible variations.

One (standard, 55-gallon, oak) Barrel
Of Sweet Corn Mash

50 gallons of warm clean water (90-100 degrees)
25 pounds of medium grind (No. 4) yellow-hybrid
    cracked corn
30 pounds of pure cane sugar
1-2 quarts of unsulphured molasses
1 pound block of bakers yeast

Getting Your Supplies Together
The Barrel

A fifty-five gallon oak barrel will do you fine. These can often be obtained from wineries and distilleries, for prices that vary greatly according to their supply and demand and how good the buyer's rap is. Other hardwoods, such as hickory, alder, ash, or poplar make suitable mash barrels, but are harder to come by. Make sure the barrel dosen't have any cracked staves. If it is dry, and not damaged, it may look like it could never hold water due to the spaces between the staves. But do not become discouraged, it can be cured, most likely, by soaking the barrel. It may take several days with cold water. Warm is much quicker, but the barrel should season up and not leak a drop.

Also make double sure that there is no metal in the barrel that is going to come in contact with the mash. That is very important. A galvanized nail buried in the wood can poison the whole batch with zinc salts, which will not distill out. His barrels are beautiful, and the moonshiner spends a lot of time in their company, so he picks and treats them with care.

The Mash Box

You can build your own mash box that will serve you just as well. But you must build it right. Use a good hardwood for the box, preferably white oak, or hickory. Don't use fir or pine unless you want turpentine or some similarly related atrocities in your mash, and therefore also in your whiskey.

Build it with pegs, dovetail joints, hemp lashing, whatever you can come up with. Just use no nails, screws, or other metals and avoid glues or anything else that might react chemically with the mash. Make your joints and seams as tight as you can and take comfort in the fact that most cracks up to $\frac{1}{4}$ inch can be seasoned and swelled by soaking. The important things to remember are that the mash should touch no metals, and that the barrel dosen't leak.

There are other things you can do in a pinch. If you hap pen to have a fifty gallon high-fire stoneware or ceramic urn lying around, or know where to score one, then that will work wonderfully. Even glass will work, but it doesn't provide much insulation, and is subject to drops in temperature. The moonshiner likes his barrels and boxes, but in desperation, when all else fails, he knows he can get by setting a batch or two in a plastic garbage can. Oh well.

Corn

Go to the feed store and buy 25 pounds of cracked corn. Ask for a medium grind—No. 4—yellow hybrid. No chemicals, please, just corn. You might start dropping remarks around town about the chicken coop you've just finished building.

Since the mash can be almost any kind of fermented organic materials, which implies a vast variety of combinations, you've got the rest of your life to explore new recipes. After you've tried the suggested recipe, you can start experimenting with different grains and combinations of them. Try 5 or 10% rye with the corn. Or barley, with a third rye and a third corn. Each grain adds its own special quality to the whiskey. Your taste and preferences will dictate the characteristics of the blend and brew you decide is "the best." But then, plain ole corn likker has been a favorite for ages.

The Sugar

The recipe calls for 30 pounds of pure cane sugar. If the package doesn't say "cane sugar," then it's probably beet sugar, and you don't want it. Cane sugar and beet sugar have different molecular structures, and cane sugar has the kind that breaks down into alcohol more quickly when exposed to yeast—which naturally brings a smile to the moonshiner's face.

Feel free to use more sugar, more molasses, or even lots of molasses. Some moonshiners use up to fifty pounds of cane sugar for a fifty-gallon batch of mash. As for molasses, rum is made from molasses, and if you like the taste of rum, then go heavy on the molasses. In the old days—the real old days—Yankee Traders made a triangle between New England, the Caribbean and Africa. They got molasses in Jamaica, brought it to Boston where it was distilled into rum, then took the rum to Africa and traded it for slaves—which they then traded for more molasses. Today, both molasses and slaves are more expensive, but if money is no object, feel free.

If money **is** an object, consider corn syrup. Not the kind that the government used to give away in its surplus food program—that kind has all sorts of chemicals in it. Pick out the **pure** kind if you decide to use it. The moonshiner is touchier than the most devout organic eater about chemicals in his mash. Long term poisons have a way of turning into short term poisons when mixed together and run through a still. Commercial distilleries add all kinds of chemicals to their liquor. Real moonshine is pure, natural, organic.

The Yeast

The best and cheapest suitable yeast to use is the kind that bakers use. It comes in one-pound blocks, and that's just what you need for this recipe—a one-pound block. See your local baker. A lot of people are doing their own baking these days. You just happen to be doing a little more than most of them. Be careful with the yeast—it's fragile. Keep it out of the sun, or any strong light. Keep it away from heat or extreme temperature changes. Use it within a few days after buying it.

There's a lot of leeway with the yeast, too. If you can't get baker's yeast, you can use dry active yeast. This is sometimes available in bulk from health food stores. As a last resort, you can buy the yeast in little envelopes from your friendly local supermarket. This kind of thing is to be avoided if possible—mainly because it costs more. Also, something rubs the moonshiner wrong in the thought of using ingredients that come in neat little plastic packages. The moonshiner has a love for the raw materials of his craft, and a strong distaste for fancy packaging of any kind.

If you **do** use dry active yeast, it will not automatically liquify when you mix it with the sugar. You'll have to add a little warm water to get things going. Other than that, everything's the same.

Molasses

You need at least one quart of molasses. If you use molasses, make sure it's either blackstrap or pure unsulphured molasses. Go a little easy with blackstrap, it's stronger. As a rule of thumb, the moonshiner is a nitpicker when it comes to the purity of his materials. Just as copper means copper, so molasses means molasses—not molasses and sulphur. Who wants to drink sulphur—or anything that has to do with sulphur?

Selecting the Location

A smart moonshiner considers, and settles as best he can, every detail of his operation before beginning. In all phases of whiskey-making, the preparations you have made go a long way toward setting the course of the operation itself. Timing is important, and if you have to take time out during the run itself to attend to things that should have been settled earlier, you run the risk of blowing your timing, and with it, the whole show. The location for setting the mash is important, and there are a lot of angles to choosing one. Usually the working mash barrel is placed fairly close to the still, making it easier to transfer the mash to the pot. You're going to need warm water—fifty gallons of it. Ideally, the water should be 90 degrees Fahrenheit. It doesn't **have** to be that hot, but the mash will start working a lot faster if it is. On the other hand, if the water is colder than 45 degrees, the yeast will struggle to survive. This is one variable out of many. The degree of control you get over all these factors will determine the quality of the final product.

Another thing that nibbles more or less continuously at the fringes of a thinking moonshiner's mind is the possibility of getting caught. Getting caught with a fifty-gallon barrel of mash is just as illegal as getting caught with a fifty-gallon barrel of good, clear, sweet, 190-proof corn whiskey. The mash is going to have to be left alone for a period of time, the length of which can't be exactly predicted. If the weather turns cold, if the yeast is weak, if the water isn't warm enough, it's going to take longer. If everything clicks, and if the mash gets a nice dose of sunlight, you might be ready to run in half the time you figured. In any case, the mash is vulnerable for however long it takes. Smart moonshiners hardly ever set their mash in state parks. How far are you going to have to go to check your mash? How far, if at all, are you going to have to lug the mash to the still when it's ready to run? Obviously, everyone's situation will be different. Do your best and think ahead. If you're spiritually inclined, the official motto of the Boy Scouts of America makes a good mantra.

Odds and Ends

Here are a few additional supplies you're going to have to take to your location. Get a good stiff scrub brush and a box of baking soda. Find a large gunny sack and wash it 'til it's as clean as Queen Anne's lace. Bring along a large pan (4-8 quarts) and a fork.

If you've gotten it all together, and everything feels right, then say a little prayer to the god or gods of your choice, and let's get cookin'!

Preparing the Mash

First soak the corn. To do this, pour it into the gunny sack. Then tie the bag off near the top, leaving room for the corn to expand to half again its volume. Throw the bag into a tub of warm water and leave it alone for three days. This will start the corn fermenting naturally and give the mixture a healthy start.

When the grain has soaked and you're ready to set the mash, scrub out the barrel thoroughly with the brush and liberal amounts of baking soda.

Then the barrel gets rinsed out **just as thoroughly** to get rid of all the baking soda. A trace of soda in the barrel will kill your mash, so be sure about it.

Put the clean sack full of corn into the clean barrel. Pour the molasses—or malt—in after it. Now set aside at least three cups of sugar (you'll need them later) and dump the rest into the barrel. Fill the barrel with warm water—to about two inches below the top, to allow for bubbles and foam. The mash is now primed and ready to go. What you need to kick it off is the starter.

To make the starter, crumble the yeast block into a pan. Pour the sugar over it that you had set aside earlier. Now mash the sugar gently into the yeast with the fork, breaking up the larger lumps. For a few minutes nothing will happen. But watch closely. Suddenly, after about five minutes, the yeast and sugar will melt together and form a thick, foamy liquid. It's like a magic trick. The foam will thicken and swell, rising in the pan like intelligent quicksand. Let it foam and grow up to the lip of the pan, then pour it into the barrel. (You'd better not make your starter until your mash is ready, or it'll run all over the ground, like the Blob.) Stir the mixture once, gently, to spread the yeast over the surface. Then step back and reach for your Bull Durham. The mash has a life of its own now, and all you can do is watch it carefully, smell it, taste it, keep it company and whisper sweet nothings over its changing surface until the signs tell you that it is growing up and is ready to be run through the still. That moment may come as quickly as a day and a half, or, under certain conditions, may take up to a week. But when it comes, you have to know what to look for.

Fermentation

How long you will have to wait depends on a lot of things, some of them outside of your control. If the water was cooler than 90 degrees, the yeast isn't going to reproduce as quickly, and the whole process is going to get off to a slower start. If the water is cool, expect to wait longer. The yeast can vary in freshness, and **that** will make a difference. The moonshiner can't rely on clocks and gauges—that's for the Jack Daniels people. The moonshiner must depend upon his own senses of sight, touch and smell. Nothing is automated. The moonshiner hovers over his barrels like a chef. He is mindful of the subtlest changes. He knows when to act and when to leave well enough alone. He neither stirs nor jostles his mash once the yeast has been added.

Whether the mash is ready in two days or a week, and whether it's corn or some other fermentable base, the process of fermentation is the same. The yeast will consume the sugar and in doing so, emit carbon dioxide gas, and—of course —alcohol.

At the point where you add the starter, the mash is a barrel of sugar and water. Taste it. It will taste sickeningly sweet. It will be sticky between your fingers. Note the color at this point. As the sugar is used up and the alcohol appears, the mixture will lose its sweetness and take on the "dry" quality of wine. Dip your fingers in from time to time and taste, for your education and peace of mind. The laws of nature are working for you. The moonshiner takes a lot of comfort from working hand in hand with the laws of nature.

When you add the starter, it will fizzle on the surface of the mash for a few minutes—for about as long as it takes for you to finish your smoke. Then it will die away to a thin, patchy foam. In ten minutes to a half hour, tiny bubbles will appear all around the edge of the barrel in a thin white line, disappearing as soon as they surface. Look at the mash carefully at this point. Study it and remember how it looks. In a few minutes, larger bubbles will begin to appear at random points across the surface.

At first there will be just a few—bobbing up and holding fast for a while before disappearing. Little pock marks will appear in the foam as the bubbles pop. If everything is working right, in maybe an hour the bubbles will be coming up faster than they disappear, crowding each other into a thickening white foam. At this point, the moonshiner can hardly hold back a smile. Something is happening in that barrel, and that something is makin' alcohol. It **has** to. It's a good time to adjourn for a plate of ham hocks or a little while with the old lady. All is well.

If the moonshiner comes back in three to six hours, finds the area undisturbed by strange footprints, and finds the bubbles coming so fast that the mash appears to boil, his smile broadens. If he can hear the bubbles popping and fizzing from twenty feet away, he chuckles. If he bends over the barrel and feels the cool spray, like a monster ginger ale, on his weathered face, he howls into the wind. If there is no wind, or other covering sound, he probably keeps quiet. Time is part of the moonshiner's investment, and the quicker the mash comes to a strong "boil," the more time he is going to save.

When the mash really begins to work, the gunny sack will start to bob up to the surface and then down, regularly in the barrel. As the yeast works its way through the pores of the bag and reacts with the sugar, bubbles of gas will be trapped, floating the bag to the surface; then, the bubbles are released into the air, at which point the bag will sink. A bag that appears every few minutes on the surface of the mash, wallows over like a lazy whale, then sinks again, is a very good sign indeed.

Watch the building of the process. When the "boiling" seems to be leveling off, you can figure that the fermenting process is about half finished. There is now enough alcohol in the mash to kill the yeast faster than it can multiply. Also, the sugar is being exhausted, and there is less for the yeast to feed on. The fermentation will gradually slow down until the thick head breaks up into individual bubbles. Then there will be just a few random bubbles, as there were in the beginning. Finally, the large bubbles will stop coming entirely, and all that will be happening will be the thin line of tiny bubbles around the edge. The mash now is sort of milkier or creamier colored than at the beginning.

For the moonshiner, this is a critical time. The alcohol content is very close to its highest point, and noticeable to the taste. If the mash is left alone much longer, the alcohol will start to react with bacteria in the air, forming vinegar. Vinegar is good stuff, and a little slosh of it can sure liven up a plate of turnip greens, but the moonshiner doesn't want to find it in his mash barrel. He knows that a few hours one way or the other isn't going to make too much difference, but by now he's tired of waiting. It's time to start the run.

You can simplify your estimating the progress of the mash by buying an inexpensive hydrometer—the kind used by beer brewers. Float it in the mash. When it shows about 16 percent alcohol, it's time to go!

That's one way to do it; about as simple and basic a method of preparing the mash as you're likely to find. Even keeping to this basic method, though, there are some things you can do differently. In some cases, you may be able to cut a few corners without hurting your final product. But it is important to know **which** corners you can cut safely. Every moonshiner's situation is a bit different from the other man's, and it makes plain sense to use what's most easily available.

Old School

As in any art, there are the modernists, and there are the traditionalists. Moonshining has been going on for a long, long time, and many of the methods that are common now are fairly recent. Before Prohibition came along and turned moonshining into a large-scale industry, there was more emphasis on quality and less on time saving and production boosting. The traditional moonshiner, from around the turn of the century and before, supplied his friends and neighbors exclusively—and himself. He had to live with his customers, and he stood behind his product. There are still many moonshiners who go by the old ways.

In the old days, sugar and yeast were very seldom used in the mash. The corn was malted and the process relied entirely on the fermentation of the natural sugar in the corn. Usually two weeks must be allowed for the mash to ferment without the boost of sugar and yeast.

The old school method has the drawback of a lot lighter alcohol yield, as opposed to sugar and yeast. You **can** add a quart of molasses to the mash if you want, and not outrage tradition too seriously. The molasses will boost the alcohol content a little, and it will smooth out the whiskey considerably.

It's hard to find any measurable scientific advantage to the old school of whiskey making, other than the rising cost of sugar. But if you would rather take more time and do things as they were once done—and make it "like they used to make it"—then the old school might be just the thing.

MALTED CORN

The old timers still like to malt their corn first, omiting sugar sometimes and the molasses. Malting grain converts the starches into simple sugars which the yeast converts into alcohol.

First you must sprout the corn. Start with whole, unground corn seeds. Cover them with warm water, and leave them in a warm, dark place for 24 hours. Then drain off the water completely. The corn should be moist, but if there's too much water in the barrel it will begin to rot. Rinse the seeds with fresh water every day until the sprouts have grown a good two inches. A cheesecloth or screen can be used for draining. When the sprouts are ready, you should spread them in the sun or under a sun lamp to dry.

When the sprouted corn has dried, it should be ground up into a nice, chunky, granulated texture. Traditionally you would take it to the local miller who would exchange his services for yours. If you like the primitive ways, a mortar and pestle will do. Very slowly. A hand grain mill such as the Corona, or a coffee grinder will do also. Very slowly. Many supermarkets have large electric coffee grinders for the use of their patrons. If you do it that way, be prepared to explain to the manager what you're doing with twenty five pounds of cracked corn in the machine if it gets clogged.

A common way to simulate the malted flavor is to add a one quart can of **unflavored** malt syrup—the kind you'd use for brewing beer. You can find it in a dusty corner of the general store or a place which deals in beer-maker's supplies. This is not a necessary ingredient to your mash, but it adds a nice touch.

Brandies and Liquors

While traditional moonshine in the United States has been mainly associated with grain whiskey, it should be borne in mind that a broad variety of alcoholic beverages can be distilled from other organic plants and their fruits. The prime requisite is that the sugar content of the fruit or vegetable be sufficient to induce a natural fermentation process. Generally speaking, most fruits contain more natural sugar than vegetables do, hence are more often used for making brandies and liquor. By definition and common usage, the word "brandy" implies a beverage distilled from fruit, while the **word** "liquor" covers just about any drink that has been distilled from fermented plant matter.

Most brandies are distilled from pure wines, although some—considered "inferior brandies"—are made from a variety of naturally fermented vegetable matter. Cognac, for example, may be distilled from all manner of refuse from the grape plant. The most common whiskeys are made from corn, barley, oats or rye wheat. Vodka, as originally made in Russia, was distilled from fermented potatoes, although most commercial vodka made in the U.S. today is pure grain alcohol. Folks the world over have made liquor from such things as pumpkins, turnips, cabbages, or almost any available over-ripe vegetable matter. We've even heard of such outrageous desperation as distilling garbage into an alcoholic beverage!

In no way do we recommend such outlandish resources, but we would like to introduce you to some of the tastier beverages that can be fermented and distilled in accordance with the traditional moonshine techniques. In any case, whatever the origin of your liquor, the first step is always the preparation and fermentation of the mash.

Brandies

There are two methods for making fruit mash. The first is the natural fermentation method. This is basically nature's way of making wine. For example, you can fill a barrel with pure apple cider (with no preservatives added) and let it ferment naturally in its own good time. That is, without adding any ingredients like sugar and yeast to hasten the process. When it has fermented, before it starts to turn to vinegar, which you can tell with a hydrometer, and when its alcohol content has reached its peak, pour it in your still and run it off. What you'll get from this hard cider is apple jack, one of the finest fruit brandies man has ever distilled. It's downright heaven when it's heated with a bit of stick cinnamon, a few cloves, cardamum seeds, and a dab of fresh ginger root.

The second method for preparing fruit mash is to hurry it with yeast and sugar. In your 55-gallon mash barrel, add 40-50 gallons of water, then five or ten gallons of pitted, squashed, **ripe** (or over-ripe) fruit. You can use plums, peaches, pears, dates, raisins, grapes, pomegranates, whatever. Add ten pounds of sugar and a half pound to a pound of yeast. The process is the same as with corn mash, except you omit the molasses and malt. Also, you won't put the **fruit** in a gunny sack. Instead, you have to strain the fruit out through a clean cloth before pouring the mash into the still.

You can use your imagination to combine various compatible fruit flavors to produce some exquisite taste treats. There's no doubt about it, fruit brandies are the nectar of the gods! Near the end of this book you'll find more about various kinds of spirits that folks have concocted and gotten wasted on all over the world.

CHAPTER FIVE

THE COUNTRY RUN

The process of distilling the pure whiskey from corn mash, is a fairly exacting craft that will call for you to be on top of things for an extended period of time. Once you start heating the mash, and consequently start the run, you don't have much time or leeway to do anything but tend the still. There might be long periods of rest, but you never can tell when they will end, so you leave the still site at the risk of blowing the whole operation. It would be wise to check, and double check, every aspect of your situation—from equipment, to the weather, and everywhere in between before you start your run. Be sure that everything is ready and in good working order.

THINGS TO HAVE READY
The Flake Box, or Condenser

First, make sure your condenser is properly set up to operate. If you need to do any trenching to carry off the excess water do it well before you start the run. You won't have time once you've started cookin'. It's pretty frustrating, not to mention dirty, to be sloshing around in the mud while you're makin'.

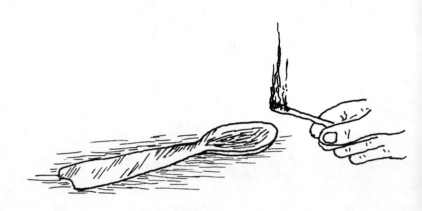

Also you will have to be sure of having plenty of water available to cool the condenser for possibly days at a time. A trial run with your flakebox is a good idea. If your condenser is wooden, it will swell the barrel and tell you if the water supply will last, and provide enough circulation to cool the vapors. Play around with the circulation of cold water into the barrel and get the rate of flow adjusted so that the water fills the barrel at the same rate it leaves, keeping the water level at the same height.

Fire Wood

You'll want to have a good supply of wood handy. Two or three runs could use up to even a quarter of a cord. Since temperature control is a vital factor in making a good batch of corn likker, you'll want a variety of shapes and sizes, possibly even different kinds of wood, dry, stacked, and ready. Generally most hardwoods are best for a steady, controlled flame. Dense western madrones and manzanita and eastern oaks are especially good for maintaining a steady, even, hot flame. These, when properly prepared and cut to several different widths and lengths, can be tossed on the bed of coals and, voila', you have the desired flame.

Every geographical area has its own unique kinds of available firewood. If you heat your home by wood you'll know pretty much what to use. If not, ask around. Do some research in the library. You might want two or three varieties of slow and fast burning woods to give you the degree desired. It would be far better to work an extra hour cutting fire wood and not use it than not to have enough. There will be no time to run out into the woods with your axe by the time you run low on wood.

Clean Equipment

The quality of your product is going to be dependent in part upon the cleanliness of the still and condenser. While your mash is fermenting is a good time to be scrubbing down your equipment thoroughly with baking soda and a stiff scrub-brush. And then, of course, rinse thoroughly. This applies to the buckets (or whatever) for moving the mash to the still, catch bottles, and naturally, the still.

Miscellaneous Tools and Supplies

Bring along a good supply of matches, a clean tablespoon, and a proof vile, all required for the Proof and Purity tests described in this chapter.

Don't try to start your run without the tools you'll need for opening, and assembling and disassembling the different components that make up the still. Also whatever clamps and fittings you've rigged for your particular still. Some hot pads, pot holder or heavy leather gloves, will save many burns and curses. The equipment gets **HOT!** Bring light for the late hours as any run is very likely to continue through at least one night. So be prepared for some time spent with this project. Bring something to smoke if you need it, coffee, and some grub of course. Incidently the firebox can serve as a wonderful oven for baking spuds and things like that.

Mash

It seems pretty obvious that in preparing for a run, the mash is the main determining factor as to when to start. It should be fairly close to the still, or have some sort of method worked out so the mash, when ready, can be easily transported to the kettle. As all the action on the surface of the working mash barrel begins to slow, and the mash is reaching peak alcohol content, all your equipment, cleaned and ready, should be there and just waitin' for some action.

SETTING UP
Still Assembly

Set all of the parts of your still together, clean as a whistle. All valves checked? All shut? Sure would be awful to be filling your pot and then discover, after inquiring about the snails pace progress you're making, that the last twenty gallons of mash have run right through the still and onto the ground, as fast as you can fill it, and that, because you forgot to close the drain valve at the bottom of the pot. Listen to the voice of experience. Be prepared. After your first run, you'll know more of what to expect the next time. Every run you do will have its common points. Every run you do will be different. Not a whole lot of boredom in this game.

Proceed to assemble the remaining still parts, connecting all fittings tightly (being careful not to strip any fittings.) Use either the rubber or cardboard gasket you've made for the cap-to-kettle connection. Secure the cap in place and close for the duration of the run. Instead, you can use a paste of flour and water to seal this joint. To do this simply make a dough, thinner than for bread, and lay globs along the lip of the pot and set the cap firmly in place, squeezing out excess glop, and clamp tightly. As the still heats up, the flour and water paste dries, and makes a pressure tight, self sealing gasket. You must, logically, bring some flour if you decide to go this route.

70

If your mash is worked off, and your equipment is ready, it is time to start. You can't fool around now. It's only a matter of hours before the mash begins its next metamorphosis. It will either begin to turn the alcohol to vinegar, heaven forbid, or it will now be transformed into the country cure-all.

When running only half a barrel at a time, it is a good idea to begin running the first half just a little before the mash has completely stopped working, say two or three hours. This way, by the time you're finished with the first and ready for the second half, the 'ripe' mash will not have been waiting so long and will have less of a chance to go sour. O.K.? Let's do it!

THE RUN

Pour the first half of the mash in the inlet hole to fill your still. Remember to leave some room (at least four inches) between the mash level in the pot, and the top of the side walls. This is, again, to ensure that the boiling head and foam, while cooking, will not get up into the cap and connecting tubes thus clouding the batch and blowing it.

The Fire

Begin by building a roaring fire in the heater box. You first have a large volume of cold liquid to heat, which will take same time. Second, it is best to have a good bed of coals established by the time the brew begins to reach its running temperature. This will enable you to throw a stick or two in, have them ignite quickly, burn evenly, and, combined with draught control, should give you a pretty good hand over the situation.

Never build a fire under an empty pot, or leave it on the fire between loading and draining, for more than a few minutes at a time, if at all. This could very easily result in your beautiful copper still falling apart before your very, crying, eyes, as the solder melts, leaving you with a pile of odd shaped sheets of copper, and not even some hooch to drown your sorrows in.

It might take anywhere from two to six hours to get the full kettle up to the running temperature (173). This is one of the few times during the run where you will have some safe time to eat or take care of last minute business. You can leave for a while, but it is never good to be away from the still for more time than is absolutely necessary. Keep a close eye on that fire.

The Working Condenser

Fill the condenser and regulate the flow now. The trial run, when setting up the equipment, should have given you some idea of what to expect. Play around with it till it is just right and check it periodically during the run. If something should mess up and the condenser goes dry, the alcohol will continue on out of the condenser as a vapor and escape into the air, doing nobody much good at all and, in fact, defeating the purpose of the venture completely.

The Country Run

As the mash approaches runnin' temperature, you'll want to start cutting the flame back gradually, giving less and less heat as the temperature gets closer to 173 degrees. This is a very critical time in the run. If you don't cut back your heat fast enough, you could overshoot the mark immediately, getting off to a poor start if not blowing the whole show. If you cut back too fast and too much, it might take hours to regain control and bring it back up to runnin' temperature. Practice makes perfect. If you don't have any practice behind you then keep in mind the principle and object of each phase of the operation and use your head. There is no magic involved. Just a goal, method, and the means.

The liquid is getting hot now and is starting to give off steam which has no place to go but through the system. The steam will begin to build up pressure and move slowly through the tubes, seeking its way into your bottle. You can follow the progess here by simply feeling the connecting tubes and different parts of the still with your hands. Since copper is such a good conductor of heat, you will be able to know exactly how far and fast the vapors move through the apparatus. If they are moving more than an inch every five or ten minutes, chances are that you are heating too fast.

One old trick for marking the progress of the steam to the condenser at the beginning of a run is to take candles or slabs of butter and stick them on the connecting tube just as it enters the condenser, and at various places in between if desired. This way, when the tube gets hot (and the tube gets **HOT**), the wax will melt, and the candle will fall, alerting the moonshiner that the vapors have entered the cooling box and are therefore condensing, and that the whiskey will soon begin to drip and all is well.

By the time the steam has pushed its way into the flake box, and has begun to condense, the liquid firewater is collecting up the low curves and dips of the 'worm' as it twists its way through the flake box and into your bottle. As the flow of steam is steady now, or should be, the remaining pressure and steam must get by the liquid blocking the tube in the low spots and makes a sort of rhythmic glug—blub-blub—glug sound, which you can hear by placing your ear next to the end or tail of the tube.

If you have got your head that close to the end of the tube, and can hear the stuff gurgling, then you will undoubtedly notice, without forewarning, that there is a particularly sweet and certainly heavenly scent breathing gently from this wonderful contraption, which by now has taken on a character and life of its own. Looks sort of like the tin man from Oz. Odd? Wait till one night, after two or three consecutive nights of fire tending and extensive sampling, you find yourself answering questions and debating relevant subjects, only to suddenly realize that there is no one there but you and your bud---uhhh-- I mean still.

Not too long after the glugs and smells will come the first drops. They are probably water from rinsing the coil just before the run, and any moisture which condensed during the heating of the kettle. The drops will come slowly, at first sporadically, and then gradually develop into a pattern or rhythm of sorts. Not a metronomic, steady rhythm, but a combination of steady drips and a short light 'piss' or stream. Moderate dribbles.

All of a sudden one of these drops is going to be the real stuff and you can bet your beans—there's no mistaking it!!

THE WHISKEY

Just to be safe (and I can hear the groan of disapproval and arguments now), on the first run, and especially the first time you use your shiny new still, let's throw away the first ounce into the fire. It should toss up a nice flame, yup, that's skunk juice alright!

Start collecting it and get ready to run some tests to gauge 190 proof whiskey. You'll need this information to compare to all your later Proof and Purity tests when cutting your brew and deciding on the strength and volume desired. From here on, you will be running these P + P tests periodically throughout the run. If you're into it, a little book of notes might prove useful at first, or even possibly provide a log to compare future runs and observations.

First, you should understand the difference between Proof and Percent. It could be confusing if these terms were not understood. The easiest way to remember is that the percent (say, for example, 50 percent) of alcohol, in a liquid, is exactly that (50% or half the volume). That is very simple but many folks tend to confuse the proof of a beverage with the actual percentage of alcohol in it, and vice-versa. The proof is simply twice the percent. Fifty percent alcohol in a drink is 100 proof. Simple, isn't it?

Meanwhile, the whiskey is spurting regularly and steadily into your jug. If everything has gone right so far, what you are now catching is 190 proof (95%) ethanol. It is as strong as it will ever be. A drop or two on the tongue will verify this last statement. That is the first and most obvious test, also the most inaccurate, and should prove to be the most frequently used test. At the same time, it gets more and more inaccurate each time it is done. Taste and experience the new potion and then let's get down to business. It may seem like a good time to celebrate, but you've only just begun. A "Yaaa-hooooo' or two would be appropriate now. A taste or two won't hurt. But you must keep your wits about you-the whole batch is at stake.

Again, the first drops and up to the first pint or so that you get should be 190 proof. After that, the proof should start decreasing steadily as the run progresses. In order to

keep track of the diminishing proof, you can now take the P +
P tests with the 190. Using the results as a base, you can compare the rest of the test results taken at regular intervals and
estimate the approximate proof of the stuff. You'll need to
know the proof to determine when to do your second and
third (if any) runs, when to quit, and how strong you want it.

THE P + P TESTS

The first three tests will involve igniting the sample. The
procedure is the same, but you will look for three different
reactions. NOTE: **ALL** tests should be done with a sample
taken directly from the tube and not from the collective catch
in the bottle. These comparative tests should be done at timed
intervals (every 10-20 minutes or so), and with a fresh sample
each time.

P+P Test No. 1

Take a clean tablespoon and bend it so it will sit on a table with the bowl of it level. Fill it with a test sample. Then light a match and bring it up slowly to the spoon. You should notice here how easily the alcohol ignites. 190 proof will have no problem at all. Any sample which is of 100 proof or less, will not ignite in the spoon. It follows then that as it gets more difficult to light the sample, the proof would get proportionately lower. If you can not ignite the sample with at least three matches then you can easily assume that it is less than 100.

If you wish to know how close a sample which will not ignite is to 100 proof, pour a fresh sample on a flat surface like a clean plate. If you can get it to light here, then it is 75-to-100. The sample would be below 75 proof if it would not light, spread out over a flat surface. This means that more than half of the total volume of the sample (and consequently everything the still is now producing), is something other than whiskey. Although the sample obviously has some alcohol in it, it is the lowest grade, and that "something other than whiskey" that it's mixed with is undesirable, to say the least, in your liquor.

P+P Test No. 2

Using the same procedure as in the beginning of P+P No. 1, ignite fresh test sample. Notice the color and clarity of the flame. Pure 190 will burn a steady, pure blue flame. The color should be light and almost transparent, but even. Any shades of yellow around the edge of the flame would indicate impurities in the sample. A heavy yellow "beard" on the flame would mean a heavy fusel oil content, and that the sample should be considered toxic—unfit for human consumption—yechhhhh! This stuff is commonly known as 'popskull' for the enormous discomfort generously doled out to the cranial vicinity by the "yellow bearded demon." Very similar to having an eight pound splitting maul planted in your forehead.

P+P Test No. 3

Again igniting the test sample as before, observe how long the flame burns. Time it. The longer it burns, the higher the proof. The shorter it burns, the lower the proof. Mark down the time for the first sample (190) and use it as a base marking the times for the rest of the samples taken at regular intervals.

P+P Test No. 4

For this test, catch about a teaspoon or so of the 190 proof juice in thepalm of your hand. Rub your hands together, spreading the sample all over your hands. Hold your hands at arm's length with palms facing you. Slowly bring your hands towards your face and inhale slowly and gently. Notice at what point (how far your hands are away from your face) you can smell the alcohol evaporating from your hands. It will be X number of inches for each test. Keep a record of this and the results of your other tests for the first few times and you'll discover a feel for it. In a short while you should be able to guess the proof of a sample, using this method, with amazing accuracy.

P+P Test No. 5

For this test you'll need a clean "proof vile." This is a small clear glass bottle (1 oz.) with a tight cap. Fill the vile about half full with the test sample. The whiskey should be as clear as the clearest water. Crystal pure and colorless. Now give the vile a vigorous shake or two, and hold it level or set it on a table. As the bubbles from the shake disappear, a chain of uniform bubbles lines up in a circle around the inside of the vile, on top of the sample, resembling a "string of pearls." This chain of bubbles is known as a "bead." The bead of a sample is graded according to: 1. uniformity - all the same size, shape, etc. 2. size - the larger the better. 3. duration - how long they last. As you probably guessed already, the higher the grade, the higher the proof. 190 would hold longest, the beads being identical in size, and being the largest. Also, as in the other test, samples that hold no bead at all indicate less than 100 proof. Pretty simple now, isn't it?

Cutting And Proof Control

As already mentioned, the first stuff to come out should be close to 190 and decline as the run progresses. As all the catch from a particular run is mixed in your jug, it will "cut" or dilute itself as the steadily weakening spirits are mixed. A sample from the collective catch, your jug, will always be stronger than a sample from the worm at that particular time.

A good cut for your whiskey would have it over 100 proof, but palatable enough so as not to remind one of paint remover working over an old chair as it sears down your throat.

This would put a good batch somewhere in the vicinity of from 110-130 proof. This suggested "ideal" range for the entire batch, coincidently, is right about where your catch bottle would be if you stop catching when the tube sample tests out at 100p. In other words, the collective sample is always stronger than the worm sample, thus insuring a batch proof of 110 —or more when the worm proof is stopped at 100.

You can make your whiskey as hot or as mild as your taste prefers. Since everybody has a right to his own opinion about how good whiskey should taste, you're pretty much on your own when it comes to deciding what proof your white mule should be. Try the previously suggested proof first, and adjust to your taste accordingly.

What you have collected so far is first run "green" whiskey. It's drinkable, and according to the fast-buck boys of Prohibition days, it's "sellin' whiskey." But the self-respecting moonshiner is concerned with quality. And he seldom stops after one run.

Reruns or Doublin'

To properly finish the distilling of good corn whiskey, the entire batch you collected from the first run should be "doubled." This means you're going to further distill and refine your product. Doublin' makes for greater purity, mellower taste, simply better moonshine. You're going to lose just a little volume, but if you're going to be a true moonshiner,

you'll be more interested in quality than quantity. Many makers will distill their whiskey three times to get it smooth and pure.

The way to double your whiskey is to open the inlet hole on your pot (being careful to let the pressure off easy), and to pour your entire first-run catch back into the played out mash. Seal up the inlet hole. You are going to extract it again. The process is the same. Very simple.

The alcohol, already distilled from the mash once, is going to react a little differently this time. It's already seen the outside world and it's once removed. It is more highly concentrated alcohol than before, and a higher grade. It will remain mostly at the top of the mash, for it floats on water, and will consequently vaporize more rapidly. It will fill your jug faster and it will hold a higher proof longer. This time, you might get another half pint or so of 190 before the proof starts to decrease. It might fill your jug with more of a stream than a dribble this time, using the same amount of heat, and therefore takes less time.

This also means when the proof starts to diminish, it drops off a lot faster than the first-run whiskey. Because of this you should take your P and P tests more frequently (every 5 or 10 minutes or so).

When the proof test says it's time to quit, then your product should be another grade higher, considerably smoother and definitely purer. You might have a decrease in volume, but anything you lose is something you didn't want.

Third Run

This is good whiskey. It'll do the trick and it won't make you sick. Nothing to scoff at and possibly something to brag about.

But if that flame of the connoisseur, be it a flicker or an inferno, persuades you to make the finest on the block, then it's time to do the third run.

And the third verse is the same as the first—or second. You pour it back in and you take it back out. And along with all these other amazing coincidences, it will come out three times faster and hold three times longer at 190.

Cleaning Up

No matter how much you've sampled, no matter how blurred your world is, no matter how tired and hungry you are, there are certain things that really must be done to secure your equipment before you start the party.

Kill your fire. Otherwise you'll scorch the mash in the pot, making it nearly impossible to clean.

Shut down the water to your condenser and empty the barrel.

Disassemble all the parts of your still. Empty out the sour mash from the pot. It's best not to pour it out on the ground or into the creek. The slop stinks like the devil, not only fouling your nest, but also creating the danger of a bust. The odor is most distinctive. Every revenooer knows that smell. Why lead him right to your still?

Rinse out all the parts of your still with water before it gets crusty and hard to clean. Scrub out any burned sediments or scum. If you don't do it right away, you'll have a big job on your hands later. Use baking soda and a good scrub brush, then rinse **everything** thoroughly.

Flush out the condenser tube with clear water. Then fill it completely with vinegar or with the played-out sour mash, and cork both ends of the tube if you plan to store it for awhile. This little move will prevent the buildup of "blue vitriol" (crystalline cupric sulfate), a most undesirable deposit to have in your still!

O.K., those are the necessities. Depending on how safe you feel about leaving your equipment at the makin' site, you're free to go your way.

Have a nice evening. Bear in mind that even if you're an individual who can really handle his hooch, moonshine is more powerful than the stuff you've been drinking from the local gin mill. Go a bit easy until you learn how much mountain dew you can handle before you knock yourself lower than a buckwheat flapjack.

CHAPTER SIX

BOTTLING AND AGING

Since mountain dew evaporates pretty fast, you'll want to get it tightly bottled up soon after your run. And since green corn likker can taste pretty hot, we'll tell you about a few tricks for aging the stuff to take the sharp edge off the flavor. As a common rule, the longer whiskey ages, the better it tastes.

Not that green first-run corn likker isn't drinkable. **Far from it.** But it gets smoother as it ages. There are several things you can do to improve the taste of your 'shine.

First, you should make a simple filtering system, using coneshaped filter papers like the Melitta coffee maker uses. Make a triple-decker sandwich of charred white oak or hickory chips between three of these papers in a funnel, run the whiskey directly from the condenser through the filter into your jug. The biggest problem you'll have with this device will be in finding some good dry white oak or hickory, both of which are eastern woods, long used for making furniture and tool handles. There's not that much of it around these days, but if you can get ahold of an old oak or hickory axe handle or a busted chair, you can whittle off a pile of shavings with a pocket knife. Grandma'd probably turn over in her grave if you carved up her old spinning wheel. You'll figure something out. Put the chips in an oven or a frying pan and heat them until they start to smoke—almost until they catch fire. Be careful not to ignite the chips. Just brown them.

You'll need enough chips to make two or three layers about half an inch thick between the filter papers. Put the filter in a big funnel and let the whiskey flow through. The juice will take on a slightly reddish tint—sort of like commercial whiskey. Most fusel oils or impurities, if any, will stay in the filter. The whiskey will taste softer.

One triple set of filters ought to be enough for a fifty-gallon mash run. If you're making more than five or six gallons of whiskey, you'll probably want a fresh filter system.

Bottling

As to the bottling of your product—a word to the wise. There's something like a triple federal rap if you get caught reusing commercial liquor bottles. Of course, if you're makin' illegal whiskey, you're in trouble anyway, but why compound the rap? Besides, who wants to put new moonshine in old bottles?

You can bottle your corn likker in your five-gallon mixing jug if you want to. It should have a tight-fitting cap. You may find it a bit awkward pouring from a 5-gallon jug into shot glasses, in which case we'd recommend smaller jugs or bottles (or larger glasses). Whatever you put it in, be sure it's clean. There's nothing that brings a moonshiner down faster than makin' a crystal clear batch of pure corn spirits, then seeing little specks of crap floating in it from a dirty bottle. Good moonshine is always clean.

Clear glass 12-ounce beer bottles make handy containers for your whiskey. They can be tightly sealed with a bottle capper (which is easy to find and buy). It's an ideal size to carry around in your overalls at a pig roast or square dance. And it can compare in alcohol content to about a fifth of commercial whiskey, or get eight of your friends as drunk as hooty-owls.

Folks in the mountains of the South like to put up their squeezin's in big-mouth pint mason jars—the kind grandma used to use to put up her peach preserves and canned black-eyed peas. If you're into nostalgia and tradition, by all means use them. They seal up nice and tight.

Ceramic or crockery moonshine jugs are nice, too, if you can find them. There are even some nice little wooden wine kegs on the market with wooden spigots, but many of these are lined with paraffin wax, which you don't want. Be sure wooden kegs are hardwood. In the old days, the moonshiners usually kept their private family batch in the "teedum barrel." That was the best stuff off the still, kept around for special occasions. The teedum barrel was usually an "aging" barrel, too, which means it was oak with the inside charred.

Charred oak barrels provide the most effective aging for moonshine. Hickory works fine, too. The thing is, you see, whiskey won't age one bit in a glass container in a thousand years.

But given some time and a good barrel, maybe a dry cellar and a good batch to start with, you can come up with an outrageous keg of some fine moonshine. Many strange and wonderful things will be taking place over those aging years, or months, whatever the case may be. The traditional white oak barrel, aside from the color (one of the identifying and common characteristics of aged whiskey), will impart flavor and tannin substances to the whiskey.

Another amazing thing that happens is that any water, given enough time and the right climate (say a dry cellar), will evaporate through the wood, increasing the alcohol content proportionately. The average rate of increase of proof in aging whiskey is about one proof per year. This might not sound like a very good annual interest rate, besides the fact that you are losing volume at the same rate that the proof increases, but consider the fringe benefits! Once again we are assuming (or more rightly, hoping) that you are striving to make the finest spirits you can produce. And aging assures the finest.

Bottle Aging

There is a trick you can use if you can't get the aging-barrel trip together. Put a handful of charred chips of white oak or hickory right into the bottle if you expect to have the whiskey around a little while. You see, the oak actually absorbs the fusel oils out of the whiskey so it accomplishes the same thing—to a lesser degree as in a charcoal barrel. It will cut the charp edge and any smell of sour mash. If your likker still has that edge or that smell, it's a bad batch. You might try filtering it one more time through the charred oak chips. It will go down the throat a lot easier. The more exposure the moonshine gets to charred oak, the better it will "age."

Barrel Aging

Aging in an oak or hickory barrel is the best way to improve the flavor of your whiskey. It takes a bit of doing, but it's well worth it. See if you can find a good barrel that doesn't leak. A five or ten gallon capacity should do it. The last Whole Earth Catalogue or Mother's General Store (Box 506, Flat Rock, North Carolina 28731) will lead you to places to buy them. Prices for new ones are running, at this writing, from about $15 to $35.

What you'll do with the barrel is to first remove the top three hoops and take off the lid. Get a good bed of hot coals going in a fireplace or barbecue pit and chuck them inside the barrel. Rotate the barrel slowly, and keep replenishing the hot coals until you have charred about a quarter inch deep on the inside of the barrel. When you see the charred area starting to crack and split, you've done enough. That's one way. You could use an oxy-acetylene torch, or just keep burning old newspapers in the barrel until it's nicely charred.

Draw the top of the barrel back together with a rope and fit the three hoops back in their original position—with the lid in place. We don't mean to make it sound all that easy. Removing the hoops and lid, then replacing them, is a bit of a chore that will call for patience and ingenuity—maybe even some special cooperage tools. An old auto leaf-spring can be helpful in providing a hard edge to drive the hoops down into place with a hammer. When you're done, you've got a really fine old traditional aging barrel.

Soak the **outside** of the barrel in water to seal it up tight again. The warmer the water, the better. Cold water works all right. It's just slower. After charring the barrel, nothing but whiskey should go inside.

You'll need a couple of holes (called bung holes). One near the edge of one end, another on the side in the center. Now you're ready to start aging the whiskey. Pour it into the barrel and seal up the holes. Start kicking it around. Shake it. Turn it. Jostle it. Move it. Rock it. Roll it down the stairs. Every time you walk by it, give it some action.

We've heard tell of folks tying the aging barrel to grandma's rocking chair. As she sat and rocked, the whiskey sloshed around inside that charred oak barrel, getting mellower every minute. It's a fact: the more it sloshes, the more it's aging—and the more it ages, the better it gets. Maybe you'll be one of those moonshiners who can put aside some of that corn likker and let it age a few years. Most of us aren't that patient.

There's a story about an airplane pilot over in France. During the first big war he helped out some French folks, so they gave him their grandpa's old teedum barrel that contained 100-year-old brandy.

Now, it seems his plane crashed on a deserted island. All he had was the fine old barrel of brandy. A few days later, when a ship came along to rescue him, he staggered and waved his rescuers away, shouting, "Go away! I'm not finished yet!" Who can blame him?

Some enterprising moonshiners have used their inventiveness to design "artificial aging machines" to keep whiskey moving in the barrel. With such devices, they can "age" whiskey the equivalent of six months in only three days' time. The idea is to figure out a way to rotate or agitate the barrel effortlessly. One way is to float the barrel in a tub of hot water. A firebox under the tub provides enough steam to penetrate the barrel and swell the wood. An overhead motor with a belt running down around the barrel keeps it rotating night and day until the moonshine is smooth and mellow.

You might try putting the barrel in a gently agitating washing machine filled with hot water. Whatever?

The main points to remember about bottling and aging are: clean bottles, tight caps, charred hardwood barrels, keep it moving— and the longer it ages, the better it gets.

Enjoy!

STEAM
ENGINE
TEMP.

MADE BY
KAPALKO
BADU

CHAPTER SEVEN

KITCHEN STILLS

Now that you've learned all about how the traditional moonshiner makes his tiger sweat, you'll be amazed at how clean and simple it is to run a batch in the comfort and privacy of your own kitchen. The equipment is simpler and easier to get together. You won't have to put out as much cash. It won't take nearly as long. It's a lot safer, since you have better control over your heating and cooling systems. It's compact. Compared to the complicated operation of the country still, kitchen whiskey is as easy as baking a cake. You can do it in one evening.

After a hard day at the cookie factory, just drop by the health food store on your way home, and pick up your ingredients. Bring 'em home. Kick off your shoes and get out of your city duds. Set up your still pot and condenser on the stove and kitchen sink and start cookin'. You'll have time to watch a little TV while the whiskey's makin'. During commercials, you can slide in to the kitchen to see how things are going. By bedtime you'll have enough whiskey for the group when they drop in next weekend. And a night cap as well.

It's true, the kitchen still is the best thing since sliced bread. It's quick, it's clean, it's cheap, it's safe, and there's not much chance of calling attention to your activity. Of course, there will always be the tell-tale stench of sour mash

in the air around. And you may be seen coming and going with some rather peculiar apparatus. But by and large, you'll find the kitchen run to be a bit of a breeze, and free of much of the paranoia that is likely to accompany the outdoor moonshiner. Of course, your yield will be less with a smaller still, but then it's easier to run more often than in the country. And, for cappers, your corn squeezin's will be every bit as good—if not better—than the whiskey made in the woods.

One word of caution to those who choose the kitchen still. There are principles and guides in the material on country stills that will assure the success of your kitchen run. The point is, that indoors or outdoors, you're going to be a moonshiner. You need to know all the basics of moonshining—so read it all before you begin. 'Nuf said. Let's get on with it.

Things to Have Ready
Lay Out

Let's assume your kitchen has a stove and a sink with cold running water. A gas stove is going to serve you better than an electric stove, simply because you've got finer control of your heat.

An electric stove will work fine if you've got the hang of controlling the burners.

Mash Barrel

You'll need a pot or tub in which to ferment the mash. It can be oak or other hardwood, crockery, glass or, if nothing else, plastic. Don't use any metals, such as aluminum, iron or galvanized metals, as they will cause a chemical creation of toxic salts and impurities that can produce deadly popskull instead of pure liquor. The capacity of your mash barrel should be in proportion to your still capacity.

Pot

The working principle behind every still is the same. The ideal pot for the kitchen still is a 4 to 6 quart pressure cooker of copper or, most likely, stainless steel. You'll need to make a couple of simple modifications in the pressure cooker to convert it to a working still pot, but they are easy to make.

First off, you'll need to pop out the pressure release valve on the top of the lid. Here, a hole the size of your copper tubing should be made and a piece about a foot long attached at one end to this hole. This provides the exit route for the vapors as they leave the pot. Get yourself a set of fittings from a plumbing or air conditioning supply outfit, or anybody who deals with copper tubing. Secure one end of the tubing to the lid of the pressure cooker. On the other end secure a standard female fitting. This can be done with a couple of small wrenches and a little care.

Curve the tubing gently in the middle to a 90-degree angle. The other end of the tube will attach to your slag box.

If the cooker you find has a temperature gauge, fine. If there is a pressure gauge on the lid of your pressure cooker, remove it and replace it with a temperature gauge with a range that includes from 100 degrees F. to 212 degrees F. You can pick up one of these at a hardware store, restaurant supply or auto parts shop for just a few bucks.

If you use an old pressure cooker for your still pot, make sure the gaskets are good so it will seal up tight. Scrub it clean. There is your pot, with only one or two small modifications. See how easy?

Slag Box

The principle of the kitchen slag box is the same as that described for the country still. Essentially, it works to further condense and purify the alcohol vapors as they travel from the pot to the coil. The kitchen slag box can be a little smaller than the one used in the country, because you're dealing with less volume. But it must be made of copper (silver soldered) or stainless steel.

Get it as clean and pure as you can. Attach threaded fittings to your slag box to connect it between the pot and your condenser.

You can make whiskey without a slag box, but its use is highly recommended for purity and safety.

Condenser

For the kitchen, you'll need a miniaturized version of the country still condenser. You'll need enough quarter-inch copper tubing to run from the stove over to your kitchen sink, plus about six to ten feet which will be spirally coiled down into your condenser barrel with about a foot sticking out of the lower end of the barrel for catching the juice. Since the distance from stove to sink varies in every kitchen, you'll have to measure your own layout to determine exactly how much copper tubing you'll need. Better to get too much than not enough.

Set your condenser barrel on the counter next to the sink with the drain valve set in such a way that the overflow runs off into the sink. Run a short piece of hose from the cold water faucet into the top of the condenser barrel. You may have to fool around a bit with the inflow and outflow to get the water circulating efficiently. But it's a dream compared to the country run, if you don't mind the low volume.

Incidentally, as long as you're operating in the convenience of a modern kitchen, you might try dropping ice cubes in your condenser barrel during the run to increase the efficiency of the system. Again, it's sure a whole lot simpler than country moonshining.

The Mash

The ingredients for preparing your mash for the kitchen run are going to be a little easier to get together than for the country run, mostly because you'll be using smaller quantities. For example, instead of buying 25 pounds of cracked corn from the feed store, you can pick up a little bag from the health food store, which won't attract as much attention. If you're a little leery about questions from suspicious store clerks, you can buy your corn, sugar, yeast and molasses from separate stores. It's surprising how many folks are hip to the purchase of that particular combination of products. "Whatcha gonna do, make some moonshine?" they ask loudly. Some people have no manners at all.

Here's a list of ingredients for the kitchen run. It makes 5-10 gallons of mash:

5-10 gallons warm water
2½-5 lbs. cracked corn
5-10 lbs. sugar
¼ lb. yeast
1 pt. molasses (or 1 cup unflavored malt)

You'll need a small gunny sack or other equally porous bag to contain the corn. Also you'll need baking soda and a scrub brush for cleaning out your mash barrel and still before you start the run. Plus, several common kitchen items like pans, fork, spoon and such.

The mash is prepared and observed exactly as spelled out for the country run. It's just on a smaller scale. Instead of a big oak barrel, you can use a kitchen crock or tub. The adding of the ingredients and the starter works in the same order. The bubbling and foaming reactions taking place in the mash should be the same.

As with the country run, you'll put the cracked corn in a small clean gunny sack, allowing enough space in the bag when you tie it off for the grain to expand to half-again its original volume. Then soak it in warm water, until it's ready for the starter.

Remember, you don't want to begin mixing your starter (yeast and sugar) until you're ready for it—otherwise you'll have the foamy stuff crawling all over your pant legs and kitchen walls.

You'll notice when the mash first starts to work off, it will have a darkish molasses color. After a while it will take on a pale orange tint. Finally, when the mash is worked off and ready for the still, it will be a kind of milky color.

Brandy

While we're on the subject of mash, one pretty nifty way to make brandy is to pour a gallon of wine in your still pot and run it off. Be sure it's real wine, though. There are a lot of artifical wines on the market (those sweet fruit-flavored test tube beverages to which alcohol is added rather than naturally fermented) which won't do at all for making brandy.

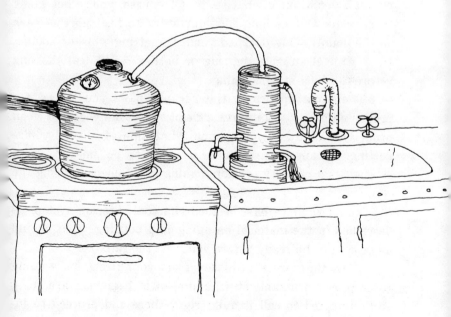

The Run

Get all your still parts clean as a whistle with baking soda and lots of rinsing. When your mash is ready, get your condenser water circulating well, then pour the mash into the pot. Remember!!! You must leave two or three inches at the top of the pot so the "puke" won't rise up into the copper tubing.

Turn on the stove burner under the pot to a medium-low heat. Watch the temperature gauge carefully. As the temperature of the mash begins to approach 173 degrees, level if off. It might be a good idea to mark a red line on your gauge at 173, just to remind yourself that if you overheat the mash, you blow the run. Temperature control is **everything** in this game. Bring it up gradually to 173 and **hold** it there. Your main occupation during this phase of the run is to watch the temperature.

If you did your homework on the earlier chapters of this manual, you'll know what to do. Of course, you're not going to have to wait as long for your stove to heat up the mash as the country boy does, so you'll be getting whiskey sooner. Have your clean collecting jug or bottles ready near the sink before the juice starts coming.

The same applies to the paraphernalia you'll need for proof and purity tests. Have a clean spoon, matches and clean proof vial handy so you'll know what kind of alcohol you're getting. Because your volume is going to be smaller, you'll be busy as a mammy possum making proof checks during the run.

You'll want to have a good charcoal filtering system as described in the material on aging and bottling. That should all be set up and ready before you start the run.

Now, the "green" whiskey from your first run is going to be pretty drinkable stuff, and a lot of beginners are going to be tempted to call it quits right there and proceed to indulge. The real moonshiner is going to resist that temptation, however, and will pour what he's collected on the first run back into the pot for "doublin's." In fact, he knows he'd end up with purer, safer, smoother juice, if he runs it a third time before shutting down his still. Sure, you'll lose just a little in volume, but after all, you're interested in makin' the finest quality whiskey possible, aren't you? Anyway, it's so easy.

Once again, you've got all that cleaning up to do before you get down to serious drinking. Otherwise you'll be running the risk of messing up your still for the next run. Keep your act together until you're properly secured.

So, there's moonshining from fire to jug. In the country, you'll be taking part in a good old traditional craft.

PART III

CHAPTER EIGHT

SPIRITS

Spirits are spirits. Alcohol is alcohol. It'll all get you loaded, if you drink enough. But there are beverages and then again there are beverages. Every area of the world has evolved its own special traditional drink—usually based on generations of experience in distilling whatever plant matter was abundant locally.

In the Mexican deserts the maguey plant, a variety of the cactus-like mezcal family, grows in great profusion. The Indians of the area long ago developed the distillation of tequila to a high degree. Tequila has become the national drink of Mexico. It is customarily tossed down from a shot glass or an equivalent swig from the bottle, with an alternate taste of salt and then lemon or lime, to enhance its character. It's hot stuff.

A veteran maker near the town of Saltillo told us that Mexicans drink tequila, not to get drunk, but to get strong. Infants are weaned on the stuff, nourishing them with "macho" experience.

In recent years, with its successful importation to other countries, tequila has become most popular in such cocktails as the Margarita and the Tequila Sunrise (orange juice and sloe-gin, or sometimes grenadine).

The people of Scotland claim to have invented the process of distilling on the fog-laden moors. Scotch whiskey is revered and imitated the world over, but somehow never equalled. This is probably due to the limestone nature of the water and the brisk air of Scotland. The old recipe itself is simple: sprouted corn and barley (the drier the better) and yeast. The secret of fine Scotch seems to be largely a matter of artful blending, although the purity of the barley used in the mash is felt to make a difference too. Seeds, husks and dirt are carefully screened before fermenting. The malted barley is spread in the sun and dried meticulously, then smoked with burning peat moss. The malted barley then rests for a couple of months. Instructions for the making of successful Scotch Whisky (not whiskey) could fill a manual of greater scope than this entire book. Somehow, nobody can make it like the Scots can. A fine 20 year old Scotch is truly the "kiss of the heather." To the connoisseur's way of thinking, it should be sipped straight. It is popular drunk on the rocks, or with soda or water. Any further dillution of a precious ancient scotch would be sacrilegious. What a shock to have heard one city lady order Chivas Regal and Coke! But that's the beauty of it. There's a drink for everybody.

The Irish also claim to have been the first to distill liquor, claiming it all started in the Emerald Isle over a thousand years ago. The word whiskey derives from an old Gaelic word "uisge," meaning whiskey, or "water of life." The main difference in traditional Irish whiskey and Scotch is that Irish mash contains, besides malted barley, a little wheat, oats and rye. Also the Irish **poteen** (a little still pot) is run three times, and the Scotch only two. Irish whiskey hasn't been produced in such great quantities as Scotch, maybe because of the high excise taxes, maybe because the distillers insist on using the traditional small poteen. Irish, too, is best as a "neat" sippin' whiskey, although in recent years it has gained popularity in

Irish coffee (with sugar and a layer of cream floating on top). The folks of St. Patrick's land are fond of Irish Punch, too. This is made by adding boiling water, lemon peel, and sugar.

There's a grand old tale that Irish folks still tell about a traveler who parked his horse at a public trough. After drinking his fill, the plug keeled over in a drunken stupor. Soon after, half of the town was at the trough, dipping out fine old Irish whiskey—until somebody called the cops. It seems that a local distiller was piping the illegal stuff through public water pipes for secret bottling, but they got mixed up and hooked into the wrong pipes. Now, they claim, the horses don't get drunk anymore, but the people sure do.

Now, the story from the ancient and mystical land of Egypt is something else again. There, instead of horses, it's camels. Here too, some Egyptians insist it was **their** ancestors who were the first to discover distilled spirits from fermented dates. This exotic brandy is called "buza," from whence comes our word **booze.** Archaeologists have recently discovered that the rectangular marble box in the king's chamber of the Great Pyramid of Giza, once thought to be a sarcophagus, was actually a receiving vat for buza, distilled in a golden still pot, perched at the apex of the pyramid, with the condenser precisely placed at the critical coordinate point of cosmic rays. Legend has it that the vibrations of this sacred buza were such that its consumption was rigidly confined to only the pharoahs of the Nile and the high priests of Ra. In modern day Cairo, buza is drunk with a dash of vermouth and an olive or a gherkin.

From the moist, tropical islands of the West Indies came a product distilled from molasses, a by-product of sugar cane, widely known as rum. Christopher Columbus brought cane sugar back to Europe before 1500. Rum has been distilled in the Caribbean since 1600. For several years, the British Navy supplied its seamen with a daily ration of rum to boost morale. When morale got too high in the 18th Century, the Lord of the Admiralty ordered the rum to be watered. This diluted version of rum was known as grog.

Rum was, for a long time, the staple drink of pioneer Americans. It was a major product of New England for generations. It is popular today for its versatility and compatibility with a variety of mixes. Since World War II, a lot of folks have developed a taste for rum and Coca-Cola. Like vodka, rum is good with vermouth, tonic, orange or tomato juice or what have you.

From Northern Europe (probably Holland or England) comes gin, a beverage originally made from barley, hops and juniper berries. Today, there's a lot of confusion about what really constitutes gin, as almost any grain spirits with an evergreen bouquet are being passed off as gin. Whatever they're putting in commercial gin these days, the only cure for a grim gin hangover is gin. Sloe gin is a cordial made from the little berries of the blackhorn bush, steeped in regular gin.

The fertile farm country of Russia gave birth to an abundance of potatoes. When fermented, these spuds provide a mash for the distillation of vodka. These spirits are traditionally freely drunk during and between meals in the cold climes of the northland. Currently a popular hooch among suburban housewives and junior executives, commercial American vodka has reached new lows in quality, as with most of the cheaper American-made distilled spirits. Modern vodka is mostly distilled as pure grain alcohol rather than organic spud juice. Who knows anybody these days who ever tasted real 'tater squeezins? There's no accounting for taste. Forty million Americans **can't** be wrong, probably. Martinis, gibsons, screwdrivers, and all sorts of soda pop mixes are popular with vodka.

than grain spirits. Exotic brandies are distilled from all manner of berries, barks, nuts, herbs, spices and flowers. The list is long. It includes bananas, pineapples, papaya, roses, almonds, lemons, oranges, vanilla, kumquats, lavendar, cloves, thyme, fennel, ginger, peppermint, elderberries, anise, dandelions and raisins, to say the least. A lot of folks just save all their over-ripe fruits in a barrel and concoct a sort of tutti-frutti brandy that can be mighty tasty.

Some more examples from around the world? Why not? Kirsch, otherwise known as Kirschwasser or Schwarzwalder, originated in Germany and Switzerland. It is made from unpitted wild cherries. It is aged in barrels lined with paraffin so as not to discolor the crystal clear liquid.

Then there's Tuica (pronounced tweeka), which derives from the Transylvania Alps. The mash is made from a rare, blood-red plum, first cultivated by Count Dracula in the 15th century. Transylvanians traditionally drink it warmed to about 98.6 degrees, with sugar and peppers.

The medieval peasants of Alsace got loaded—and **still** do —on an exquisite beverage called Houx (pronounced "who"). It is made by fermenting the cheerful holly berry, then distilling its lively spirits. It is so appreciated by the discriminating, that a bottle can seldom or scarcely be purchased for less than a twenty dollar bill. Only about 500 bottles of all the Houx made in one year ever reach the market. All the rest is drunk by its makers and their neighbors and kinfolk.

Owing to the fact that there are many more varieties of fruits and grains, there are more varieties of brandies

What About Whiskey?

Now, you're probably wondering why only about one percent of all whiskey consumed in America in this day and age is **blended straight whiskey.** According to Paragraph 37, Item 13-462A of IRS publication number 9-29S-4, a straight whiskey is defined as "those spirits having been aged for two or more years in a charred barrel under government supervision." There's some other stuff about straight whiskey that is almost too esoteric to get into. And then there's **blended** whiskey (stuff like Seagram's 7, Four Roses, Paul Jones and Old Tennis Shoe). Commercial distillers sell it cheap and still make a good profit—and still call it whiskey. By legal definition, it must contain no less than 20% straight whiskey with pure water and alcohol.

Bottled-in-Bond

Bottled-in-Bond Whiskey, on the other hand, has to be straight, and has to be aged for at least four years in a warehouse which is owned and operated by the United States Government, no less.

As you might guess, rye whiskey's main ingredient is that variety of grain called rye.

Canadian

Canadian Whiskey was originated by our northern neighbors. It is light-bodied, light-colored, and for a whiskey to bear that name, it must have been aged for not less than two years.

It was the distillers of Scotland and Ireland who first brought whiskey to America. The one important contribution to the list of spirits made by Americans was **Bourbon,** made from a mash whose primary ingredient was the sweet corn from the hills of Kentucky. By legal definition, the corn doesn't have to come from Kentucky, but if it's not made from corn mash, it's not Bourbon. Corn whiskey is the stuff traditionally made by the moonshiners of America. Likker which has been distilled from fresh cracked corn and the leftover liquid from played out mash is called **Sour Mash** whiskey. Its distinctive sour mash flavor has made it a prized drink, especially in the mountain south. An old Kentucky colonel who had a reputation for sippin' a lot of sour mash whiskey every day used to tell folks, "I ain't too fond of the taste of the stuff, but, shucks, it's somethin' to do while I'm a gitin' drunk!"

No matter where in the world spirits are made, no matter what fruit, vegetable or grain is fermented, the distilled products are all strong drink. A lot of them can be made with a simple still. They are all illegal to make in the United States. For those who want to know something about the laws governing moonshine, the next chapter will put you straight—so you'll know where you stand.

Fifty cents per gallon, thank you—or, no thank you, depending on one's point of view. It wasn't long before enterprising, cost-conscious Colonial distillers decided there was a less expensive way to produce a jug of whiskey—fifty cents per gallon less, to be exact—and have some fun doing it!

CHAPTER NINE

MOONSHINE AND THE LAW

No course on moonshining would be complete without one word of caution from the United States of America: don't.

But if you do, keep this in mind: when spirits are distilled in this country, the federal government wants to know about it, and when those spirits are bottled, sold, sipped or fondled, the government wants a piece of the action. Anything less than strictest compliance with relevant distillation and sales laws is considered a crime of major proportions. Penalties for convicted offenders may include heavy fines, prison terms and property forfeitures.

If nothing else, the government's attitude in this matter has the virtue of consistency. Imposition of excise taxes on the sale of distilled spirits goes back to Colonial days. When the New World's first saloon opened its doors in Boston in 1625, the king's agents were waiting with their hands out.

Moonshining

As far as the king's share was concerned, if the crown's revenue men could find the still, they could get their taxes. But finding the still could be something of a problem. And revenue agents, if they were prudent men, often decided it was just too risky to look. If the king's excise taxes on whiskey were as unpopular as history tells us they were, then the men who collected these taxes must have been exceedingly unpopular. Only a fool of an agent would have pursued his collection duties far from the pale of the king's garrisons. Many who did never came back, or did so in full tar-and-feathers regalia.

In short, moonshining thrived. Its status as a Colonial criminal institution vanished with the American Revolution in 1776; and for a brief fifteen years, while liberated colonists worked to put together a viable form of government, spirits were openly distilled and sold without taxes. Then, in 1794, under the prodding of Secretary of the Treasury Alexander Hamilton, Congress enacted into law an excise tax on the sale of all distilled spirits. At that time, it must be remembered, there was no income tax. Federal spending programs were financed almost exclusively through excise and customs taxes.

Whiskey distillers were outraged. Attempts to evade the new tax were widespread and immediate. In Western Pennsylvania, where for years farmers had routinely converted their surplus grains into the production of spirits, opposition to payment of the new tax quickly escalated into violence. Men who years before had defied the king's demand for payment of the whiskey tax, and then for years had distilled openly without fear of tax or sanction, had no intention of paying the tax now to an upstart government. And when the new government persisted in sending revenue agents into the area to collect these taxes, irate distillers decided tar and feathers were the appropriate response.

The agents kept coming, however. In July of 1794, some five hundred farmers armed themselves and, in their most definitive statement to date, attacked and burned to the ground the home of General John Neville, the federal government's regional inspector of the excise. This was too much for President Washington. He promptly dispatched 13,000 troops into western Pennsylvania to put down what history now calls the "Whiskey Insurrection." And that was the end of it. Not that hard-core rebels had any intention of paying taxes on their distillation products. On the contrary. There is every indication that defiance remained widespread. But confrontation had brought about a change of tactics—and retreat to an older, more durable approach to the problem of producing a tax-free bottle of booze: again, moonshining.

Moonshining is a federal crime. In fact, it's hundreds of different federal crimes woven together into a tightly knit fabric called Title 26, **Internal Revenue Code.** The relevant laws are administered by the Bureau of Alcohol, Tobacco and Firearms, an agency within the U. S. Treasury Department. With respect to alcohol, the bureau has two primary functions: regulatory enforcement of authorized distillation and sales, and criminal enforcement of unauthorized distillation and sales. The federal government's determination not to be cheated out of a sip's worth of tax is not exclusively directed at moonshiners. Regulations and controls applicable to the legal distillation industry reflect an almost hysterical concern for cheaters.

For example, anyone who operates a legal distillery is obligated by law to furnish agents of the bureau with keys to all structures on the distillation premises. These agents, in turn, are legally empowered to visit the premises and use these keys "at all times, as well by night as by day." And—
". . . whenever any officer, having demanded admittance, and having declared his name and office, is not admitted into such

premises by the proprietor or other person having charge thereof, it shall be lawful for such officer, at all times as well by night as by day, to use such force as is necessary for him to gain entry to such premises." In other words, break down the door. Further, there is a provision that if revenue agents suspect the legal distiller of siphoning off untaxed spirits through hidden pipes, the agents may summarily tear the distillery to pieces in search of such pipes. And, if still unsatisfied, the agents may "break up the ground on any part of a distilled spirits plant" in search of hidden conduits.

With hysteria at such a pitch in regard to suspected cheating by legal distillers, it should come as no surprise that illegal distillation—i.e., moonshining—leads to governmental foaming at the mouth. In its nearly 200-year battle with moonshiners, the federal government has lost all perspective on the problem. Moonshining is not a Communist conspiracy. Yet even a casual perusal of relevant laws reflect an astonishing degree of governmental paranoia about excise-tax evaders. Fortunately, there is some indication that in recent years the Bureau of Alcohol, Tobacco and Firearms has redirected its vendetta-like attention from busting moonshiners, to mushrooming problems within its "Firearms" jurisdiction—specifically, the growing illegal gun traffic among revolutionary groups. For once the government has something real to worry about. Yet, while this shift of emphasis has put moonshining on a back burner, the unauthorized distillation of spirits, on whatever scale, remains a crime, and bureau agents on the scent have at their disposal an arsenal of laws.

If you set up a still, long before that first sip passes your lips, you will have broken federal laws. The first crime is committed when the intent to distill without proper authorization assumes any tangible form, such as the purchase of any materials or ingredients; or, in some cases, even sooner, as when two prospective moonshiners discuss the details of their upcoming joint venture. Once distillation begins, you can be busted for any number of crimes, among them: possession of an unregistered still, failure to make property application for registration, failure to give proper bond, carrying on an illegal distillation operation, distilling in a place not designated by law, illegal bottling, sales, failure to pay the proper taxes, possession of illegally distilled spirits, transportation of illegally distilled spirits, purchase of illegally distilled spirits.

And so forth, ad nauseam. Each of these counts carries a potential five-year prison term and $10,000 fine. Woven in among the more obvious laws are carefully drawn, hypertechnical regulations which, if the occasion demands, can be brought to bear. For example, when revenue agents arrive at your still, they can bust you for your failure to display "conspicuously" those signs approved by the Internal Revenue Service, assuming, of course, that you have failed to display these signs.

If, during any phase of your moonshine operation, you arm yourself for any purpose, and the government can prove this, you are in for particularly severe treatment. In addition to any number of five-year prison terms arising out of your actual distillation activities, you will probably be socked with a ten-year stretch for the firearm. Unless the firearm is a machine gun or sawed-off shotgun, in which case conviction can get you an extra twenty. Not only are guns a crime, but the **Internal Revenue Code** specifically declares it a crime for any moonshiner to have "in his possession or in his control any device capable of causing emission of gas, smoke or flames and which may be used for the purpose of hindering, delaying or preventing pursuit or capture." The penalty—ten years. Shades of Al Capone. It's clear the United States wants its money, and just as clear that, over the years, there have been those willing to go to extreme lengths not to pay it.

In its zeal to collect taxes on booze and to bust moonshiners, the United States government has stretched the Constitution to its limits and beyond. At one time a person's mere "unexplained presence" at a still site could lead to his conviction of "possession" of an unregistered still—a crime carrying a potential five-year sentence. This was declared unconstitutional. The United States Supreme Court reasoned that mere unexplained presence at the still site was insufficient evidence to support a rational inference of "possession." However, as the law stands today, a person's mere "unexplained presence" at a still site can lead to his conviction on the charge of "carrying on" an illegal distillation operation. And the courts—amazingly—have held this to be constitutional. On this issue, the United States Supreme Court reasoned that anyone at the still site must have some connection with the illegal operation —manufacturer, bottler, lookout, consumer, supplier, mechanic, janitor—and that this connection, by definition, aids the business of "carrying on" an illegal distillery. The penalty for "carrying on" is the same as the penalty for "possession"—five years. In other words, if you are in or about the still site when the revenue men arrive, you had better be able to explain your presence in a way that makes sense, and the burden is on you to come forward with such an explanation. If you can't, and most people can't, you will undoubtedly face a "carrying on" charge.

Back a few years ago, when revenue agents moved in on a still near Bellport, Long Island, they found Julius Caesar King tinkering with the distillery equipment. Tyson King was holding a flashlight. Julius was too close to the action for a viable alibi. Tyson, however, said he was merely "furnishing company," and there was nothing criminal about that, was there? Yes, there was, said the court. Tyson was convicted of "carrying on" an illegal distillation operation.

When revenue agents bust a still, they try to make the bust when the still is operating in all its glory and all principals are present and accounted for. In that way, the government's problems of proof in court are greatly eased, for, as explained above, one's mere "unexplained presence" at a still site subjects him to the charge of "carrying on" an illegal distillery. On the other hand, if there is a still on your property, and you do not know about it—or, more properly put, you can "prove" that you don't know about it (and the burden is on you to prove this), you have committed no crime. The problem is, what twelve randomly selected Americans are going to believe your story?

When a revenue agent on the prowl knocked at the North Carolina home of Fred McKinley Mabe, Mabe was not home. Once legally on the premises, the revenue agent followed his well trained nose to a barn some one hundred yards distant where he found (and not to his surprise) a 250-gallon "submarine still," 23 one-gallon unstamped glass jugs containing some of the South's finest, and an assortment of sixty-pound sugar bale wrappers. When the agent returned the following day, Mabe, who was now in his house, departed with great haste through a back door, but lost a subsequent footrace with the law. A less resourceful moonshiner might have called it quits then and there. Not Mabe. It was time for an improvisation, and Mabe came up with one. As he told the court: he had been a renter on his property for the past three years (which was true), and during that time he had assumed that the barn in question was on his neighbor's land. In fact, said Mabe under oath, in all the time he had been renting there he had never set foot inside the barn and had no idea what was in there. Hardly a novel approach to the problem of explaining a "submarine still' in the barn. Yet, reasonable doubt being what it is, Mabe might have beaten the rap in spite of his attempted flight from the law had it not been for one fatal imperfection in his alibi. It seems that the **only** visible access to the barn was a well-worn path leading directly from the barn to Mabe's back door. Mabe was convicted of carrying on a distillery without posting bond, of producing spirits at a place not designated by law, and of possessing containers without stamps. Each charge carries a five-year prison term.

The would-be moonshiner need not actually reach the production stage in order to subject himself to criminal sanctions. Once the intent to distill is translated into any preparatory act, a crime has been committed. The **Internal Revenue Code** specifically outlaws possession of any "property intended for use in violating any provision of the distillation laws." It may be difficult for the government to prove this crime because intent, being a state of mind, is always difficult to prove. Yet, if you are found in possession of materials and/or ingredients for which there is no logical explanation other than moonshining, you are in trouble, because the intent to distill can be rationally inferred from strong circumstantial evidence.

Take the case of Willard and Modis Perry, two southerners with some big plans. In a two-month period in 1966 they purchased, at retail, from a little country store deep in the heart of moonshine country, 20,496 glass half-gallon jugs. Then, while revenue agents watched and waited, a man named Herbert Hoover Brown, a friend of the Perrys', purchased 13,308 more jugs at the same store. When revenue agents are on the scent, they normally do not move in until they have followed the scent right to the still. But this was too much. After Brown's purchase, agents busted the three men. No still was ever found, and probably none existed at that point in time. But the unexplained presence of 33,804 glass half-gallon jugs in the face of testimony that these jugs were a moonshiner's special, was sufficient evidence upon which to convict the three men of the crime of possessing property intended for use in illegal distillation.

Occasionally revenue agents, in their zeal to make arrests, themselves become so deepy enmeshed in the criminal activity under scrutiny that they pollute any arrests by making subsequent convictions legally impossible. If a revenue agent tries to make a buy from a suspected moonshiner, and the sale is consummated, the moonshiner can be prosecuted and convicted. However, if the revenue agent encourages a would-be moonshiner to set up a still, makes a buy, then makes a bust, the moonshiner can plead "entrapment" which, if proved, is a successful defense to the charge of illegal distillation and sales. The distinction between permissible and impermissible enforcement conduct is often a difficult one to make. Occasionally, though, eager revenue agents use tactics so blatantly impermissible that they themselves emerge as the culprits.

A case in point occurred in the early 1960's in California, far from the traditional heart of Moonshine Country. A revenue agent posing as a "syndicate" gangster approached two fledgling and obviously naive moonshiners with an offer to make large-quantity buys for thirsty underworld customers. The moonshiners took the agent to their Oakland home, treated him to a few drinks and, at a later date, sold him eight gallons of you-know-what. Largely as a result of intelligence gathered during this buy, other federal agents moved in on the Oakland still and busted the two moonshiners. Until this juncture, all moves by law-enforcement officers were within legal parameters. This distinction began to break down, however, when the revenue agent who had posed as a syndicate buyer telephoned the two moonshiners prior to their prison terms and, finding that his "cover" remained unimpaired, proposed that the three of them do a little business after prison terms had been served. Which is just what happened. After the pair emerged from prison, the agent, still in his guise, renewed his offer to buy all spirits the two men could produce. There was an agreement to this effect. Production timetables were agreed upon, and when quotas were not met, the revenue agent urged the moonshiners on by telling them, "The boss is on my back." At various times, the revenue agent offered to provide an alternative still site, still equipment and a "monkey" to run the still. Once, when production was flagging, the revenue agent purchased (at government expense, of course) and delivered to the moonshiners two thousand pounds of sugar. Then, in the final chapter of this incredible tale, the revenue agent stripped off his mask— surprise—and busted the two men on an assortment of moonshine charges. Needless to say, this was entrapment, and for this reason subsequent prosecution failed.

Cases like this are the exception. By and large, he who gets busted for moonshining will do time, pay fines and find himself victim of a little understood area of the law known as "forfeiture." This is how it works: if the government finds a still, in addition to arresting all principals, it can and invariably does seize and destroy all still materials and ingredients. One might expect this. Also subject to seizure, however, are all personal property, regardless of ownership, found at the still site, as well as "all right, title and interest" the distiller or distillers may have in the real property upon which the still sits. The land thereby seized is declared forfeited and is sold at public auction. Further, if the government can prove that traffic in and out of the still crossed other real properties whose owners knew where the traffic was going, all those ingress and egress properties are declared forfeited and sold at auction.

Does this really happen?

Does this really happen?

It can. And, at various times, it does. Though moonshine enforcement is aimed primarily at large-scale commercial production, now a fast-fading phenomenon of the Deep South, the laws can be enforced as well against the man whose only intent is to distill a few gallons of white lightning for his own solace and comfort. It is hard to see what legitimate interest the government has in outlawing private distillation of spirits for private consumption. Certainly there is a fundamental distinction between distillation of spirits for sales, and distillation of spirits for home consumption. One is a commercial enterprise historically subject to governmental taxation, while the other is, or ought to be, an expression totally within an individual's private jurisdiction. Yet, the government thus far has refused to acknowledge this distinction. It threatens alike, with the same heavy hand, the men whose livelihood is selling taxless moonshine and the man who distills it for non-commercial purposes. In fact, the intent of the busted distiller is not considered material in a court of law—which is to say that from the law's point of view it does not matter what the distiller planned to do with the booze. The crime is not distillation for sales, but distillation, period.

If the moonshiner is to find any solace in the laws, as they now stand, it will be behind the protective veil of the Fourth Amendment. This frequently invoked provision of the Constitution provides that a man's home and effects shall be free from unreasonable searches and seizures. In practical terms this means that, except on emergency, no government agent—be he common cop or revenue collection agent—may enter your home without a search warrant. Search warrants are issued by neutral magistrates upon probable cause, and probable cause grows out of hard facts, not mere suspicions. Failure of government agents to adhere to the letter of the Fourth Amendment when making a bust effectively renders any future prosecution impossible because of the rule that no evidence seized in violation of a person's Fourth Amendment rights can be introduced in evidence against him.

While procedural sanctuary behind the walls of the Fourth Amendment has saved many a distiller from the jaws of the law, and made many a lawyer wealthy in the process, this defensive remedy is not the answer to the problem of home distillation of spirits without fear of prison. What is needed, and what is long overdue, are substantive changes in those laws which allow the government to intrude its arm

127

into private areas to bust persons for crimes which have no victims. Just as the government has been forced to retreat from bedrooms, where it once pontificated on who could do what with whom and in what positions, it can be forced to retreat from kitchen distilleries. And the reason it can be forced to retreat is that the laws forbidding personal distillation of booze for personal consumption are hopelessly at variance with basic constitutional notions of privacy.

The only legitimate interest the federal government has in the distillation of spirits is in the quality control and taxation of whiskey produced for sale. Tobacco is subject to the same excise tax scheme as whiskey, yet anyone can grow his own tobacco, harvest it, cure it and smoke it without risking prison. Why should the would-be home distiller be subject to a different standard? The government's position with respect to home distillation leads to a legal paradox.

A man may grow his own grapes and from those grapes may make, through the process of fermentation, and for his own consumption, two hundred gallons of wine per year. If the wine made is 15 per cent alcohol—an average— the entire 200-gallon batch will contain, in diluted form, some thirty gallons of 100 per cent alcohol. While it is legally permissible for the winemaker to possess and/or consume these thirty gallons of 100 per cent alcohol in its diluted form, it would be a crime for him to extract, by distillation, the alcohol from the wine. This leaves the state in the position of saying: 1) it is legal to create, through fermentation, thirty gallons of 100 per cent alcohol; 2) it is legal to possess and/or consume these thirty gallons of 100 per cent alcohol in solution form; but 3) it is illegal to extract the alcohol from the solution; or conversely, 4) it is illegal to extract from the 200 gallons the 170 gallons of non-alcoholic liquid.

Do moonshine laws work?

It's hard to say. Obviously, the severity of the law provides some measure of deterrence. Yet, laws in this realm have always been severe, and there has always been moonshining in spite of them. The king of England was not able to wipe it out, and after almost two centuries of enforcement, the United States government has been unable to wipe it out.

The Bureau of Alcohol, Tobacco and Firearms reports that moonshining in the mid-1970's is a vastly reduced problem from what it was in the past. Which is to say that revenue agents on moonshine duty are making fewer busts these days. Perhaps this means fewer illegal stills, perhaps not. What does seem clear, however, is that large-scale moonshine operations are on the decline, and for a number of reasons. The bureau attributes the supposed decline to enforcement's technological advantage. Nowadays, revenue agents have at their disposal highly sophisticated equipment, specially trained dogs and airplanes equipped with sensitive heat-detection devices. These devices are such that, in scanning the topography, they can pick up temperature increases of the kind normally associated with large distillation processes, and they can pinpoint the spot from which these heat emissions are released.

Another fashionable explanation for the supposed decline in moonshining is economic—specifically, the inflationary increases in the prices of materials and ingredients necessary to produce spirits. As the prices of copper and sugar skyrocket, the price of a fifth of whiskey is bound to increase. The legitimate industry, because of its broader base, greater purchasing power and the advantage it has of being able to operate openly, is better able to keep prices down in the face of rising costs. Or so the theory goes. And, as the price of a fifth of mountain dew approaches the price of a fifth of legal spirits, moonshine sales are bound to decrease. On the other hand, as history has amply demonstrated, as long as the government imposes a tax on distilled spirits, there will be those—in their barns, in their kitchens and in their mountain hideaways—who will not pay.

And so the game goes on.

RECIPES

Corn whiskey has often been considered something of an outdoors drink, taken from the jug, glass or food jar. Even when drunk in a cozy cabin by the fireplace or potbellied stove it would probably be safe to say that most of the squirrel likker made in America has been drunk unmixed, undiluted, straight. But don't think for a minute that White Lightnin' ain't good in a mixed drink. For those who like a little variety, a cocktail or a highball now and then you'll be pleased to know, if you didn't already, that corn whiskey might be considered one of the most versatile alcoholic beverages available. Its clarity and the subtleness of its flavor make it an ideal base for a great many mixed drinks. Some drinks, of course, are better than others simply because of the gentle reactions that might result from mixing certain flavors. Such things are, after all, largely matters of individual taste, so in contemplating what to serve your friends, you're on your own. As with the preparation of your mash, you may feel free to experiment, to explore the infinite possibilities of surprising yourself and your drink partners.

To make matters a bit simpler for you in the beginning, we'll give you a good assortment of recipes for cocktails, highballs and other mixed drinks, all of which have shown themselves to be as tasty as anything you can get in one of them high-tone city saloons.

133

These are some recipes we've enjoyed in our own homes. To our way of thinking, some of them actually improve the drinks made with the traditional alcohol base. But, then again, that's a matter of personal taste.

As a rule of thumb we've found that Moonshines versatility is nearly as broad as that of vodka or rum. But, being a whiskey, it will also do something that the others can't do. Try some of these. You'll like 'em. We think you'll agree.

Just one more thing. Any good bartender will tell you that any mixed drink should contain no less than fifty percent of your alcohol base. Needless to say Moonshine can be mixed with almost any conventional drink mix, and even goes very well with some fruit juices. For some of the recipes given, you'll need a sugar syrup. An easy way to make your's is to boil one part creek water with one part sugar for five minutes. Pour it in a bottle and keep it refrigerated when you're not mixing drinks.

These recipes make about four drinks, unless otherwise noted.

BEAR TRAP

Shake, using 3/4 cup cracked ice:
   1 jigger sugar syrup
   2 jiggers lemon or lime juice
   5 jiggers pure corn likker
Strain into chilled cocktail glasses.

PLOW BOY

Stir well, using 3/4 cup cracked ice:
   1 jigger dry vermooth
   1 jigger sweet vermooth
   6 jiggers Moonshine
Add to each drink:
   1 dash orange bitters
Serve with hazelnut in bottom of glass.

POLECAT PUNCH

   1 quart Moonshine
   1 and 1/2 quarts orange juice
   1 quart ginger ale
   1/2 pint cherry soda
Makes 37 servings, 3 ozs. each.

MOUNTAIN MAGGIE

Stir well with 3/4 cup cracked ice:
   5 jiggers of panther juice (shine)
   2 and 1/2 jiggers lemon or lime juice
   1/2 jigger tripple sec
Pour into cocktail glasses, the rims of which have been rubbed with citrus lime and then spun in salt.

BLUERIDGE SKYLINE COCKTAIL

Stir well with ice cubes:
   1 to 2 jiggers dry vermooth
   6 to 7 jiggers corn whiskey
Add to each drink:
   1 dash Angostura Bitters
   A twist of lemon peel

BLOODY REVENUER

Shake well or blend into 3/4 cup crushed ice:
   3 jiggers Moonshine
   1 cup chilled tomato juice
   1 tsp. lemon juice
   1 tsp. Worstershire Sauce
   2 drops hot pepper sauce
   1/4 tsp. celery salt
   Pinch of garlic salt
Serve, without straining, into lowball glasses.

GRANDMAMMIES RECIPE

Shake with 3/4 cup cracked ice:
   1/2 jigger raspberry syrup
   1/2 jigger pineapple syrup
   1 and 1/2 jiggers lemon juice
   5 and 1/2 jiggers corn likker
Strain into chilled cocktail glasses and serve with a twist of orange peel.

MULE'S ASS (One serving)

   1 jigger white mule (shine)
   2 ice cubes
Fill a 6 oz. glass with ginger ale. Add a spiral of lemon peel over the rim of the glass.

MINT JULEP (One serving)
(100 year old recipe)

Use only tender mint leaves for bruising, and only finely shaved or crushed ice.
Chill a very tall glass or silver mug.
Wash and partially dry:
   A long sprig of fresh mint
And dip it in:
   Powdered sugar
Combine in a bar glass:
   2 tsp. sugar syrup
   6 medium sized mint leaves
   1 dash Angostura Bitters
Bruise leaves gently with muddler and blend all ingredients by stirring gently.
Pour into bar glass:
   1 jigger pure corn likker
Stir again.
Take chilled glass, pack it with ice, strain the above mixture into chilled glass. Churn ice up and down gently adding ice to within 3/4 from top.
Add:
   1 Pony Moonshine (1 oz.)
Churn until glass is frosted. Add the sprig of mint. Stick a long straw in it and start suckin'!

MOONSHINER'S DAUGHTER

   Shake, using 3/4 cup crushed ice:
      1/2 jigger grenadine
      1 jigger lemon or lime juice
      1 jigger apple brandy
      2 egg whites
      4 and 1/2 jiggers Moonshine
   Strain into chilled cocktail glasses.
Stir. Decorate with a twist of lemon peel, a thin slice of orange and a maraschino cherry.
Serve with a muddler.

OLD-TIMER (One serving)

Put into an old fashioned glass and stir:
  1/2 tsp. sugar syrup
  2 dashes Angostura Bitters
  1 tsp. creek water
Add:
  2 ice cubes
Fill glass to within 1/2 inch of top with:
  Moonshine
Stir. Decorate with a twist of lemon
peel, a thin slice of orange
and a maraschino cherry.
Serve with a muddler.

COUNTRY PARSON

Shake with 3/4 cup cracked ice:
  1/2 jigger sugar syrup
  1 and 1/2 jiggers lime juice
  2 jiggers apricot brandy
  4 jiggers white lightnin'
Strain into chilled cocktail glasses.

TURKEY COOLER
(One serving)

Put 4 ice cubes in a very tall glass.
Add:
  1 tbsp. sugar syrup
  juice of 1 lemon
Fill glasses with:
  Carbonated water
Stir and serve without delay.

TENNESSEE WALKIN' HORSE

Shake with 3/4 cup cracked ice:
  1 and 1/2 jiggers lime juice
  1 and 1/2 jiggers Benedictine
  5 and 1/2 jiggers stump juice
Strain into chilled cocktail glasses.

LOG CABIN HAPPINESS
(One serving)

Combine in a 2 oz. glass:
  Juice of 1 lemon or lime
  1 tbsp. pure maple syrup
  1 jigger corn likker
  2 dashes grenadine
Fill glass with crushed ice to within
3/4 of an inch of the top.
Add:

BLOCKADE WAGON

Shake with 3/4 cup cracked ice:
  1/2 jigger cointreau
  1 and 1/2 jiggers lemon juice
  6 jiggers white wheel (shine)
Strain into chilled cocktail glasses and
serve with a twist of lemon peel.
Add:
  1 Pony Moonshine (1 oz.)
Churn. Drink through straw.
Add:
  Pineapple strip
  Slice of orange
  Cherry

GLOSSARY OF TERMS

Bead

Refers to the uniform, "string of pearl"-like bubbles, which cling to the sides of the proof vile as described in chapter 5 (The Run) under Proof and Purity Test No. 5 on page 80

Beer

This term in the language of moonshine refers to the fermented mash when it is ready to run, or to the mash in general. See chapter No. 4 on the mash.

Blockader

An Appalachian term for moonshiner holding over from revolutionary days. Originally called such because the illegal whiskey had to run the blockade of revenooers. "Blockade likker" is one of the many versatile and varied names given to the infinitely infamous moonshine.

Blue Vitriols

Crystaline cupric sulphate. A substance formed when copper (usually the condenser) is not cleaned properly after a run. Can be seen as tiny blue metallic flakes in your whiskey. Highly toxic when taken internally and one of the biggest causes of ailments related to "bathtub whiskey." Chapter No. 5 under **Clean Up,** page 84

Boiling

The action of the mash as it ferments, producing bubbles

Booze

If you haven't figured that out yet, you can probably forget it. See chapter 8 - Spirits - under Egypt, page 109

Brandy

Alcoholic beverages distilled from a fruit base, or more specifically, spirits made from grapes.

Cap

The cap is the "head" of the still and directs the vaporized alcohol into the connecting tube and on through the system. See chapter No. 3 (The Still) under the Cap on page 38

Clouded

The milky color of a bad batch.

Condenser

The part of the still in which the vaporized alcohol is coiled, returning the firey stuff into liquid once again, explained in detail in chapter No. 3 on the still under the condenser on page 40

Connecting Tubes

Are the sections of copper tubing, either attached to their respective still parts or, with fittings, to connect the various parts of the still and serve as a passageway for the pressurized vapors throughout the system.

Cookin'

The process of running the still, from application of heat to the still pot through vaporization, condensation and catching of the Balm of Gilead.

Copper Pot

Most generally used to describe the type of still used in the backwoods in its simplest and purest form, which consists of a heating system, copper pot (or kettle), cap, connecting tube, and the condenser. More specifically referring to the pot itself which is of course covered in detail in chapter No. 3 under **the Kettle** on page 36

Distill

To remove the alcohol from a mixture containing it by evaporation. See chapter No. 2 under **Principles of Distillation** on page 23

Distillery

Obviously a place where distillation takes place.

Doubling

Is the second step of the actual distillation process and is accomplished by simply runnin' the freshly distilled spirits through the still in the same manner as the first run. Also called Second Run or doubled and twisted, guaranteed to twist yo' head. Doublin is covered in chapter No. 5 on the Run under **Reruns or Doublin** on page 80

Ethanol

Drinking alcohol.

Ferment

The natural chemical reaction of yeast converting sugar in various forms to alcohol. See chapter two under **Principles of distillation** on page 23 , and chapter No. 4 under **Fermentation** on page 58.

Fire Box

See heating system.

Flake Box

See condenser.

Fusel Oils

Mainly a mixture of amyl alcohols, they are a byproduct of the fermentation process, a most undesirable thing to have in your whiskey. It can be distilled out with a little care and precise temperature control and is responsible for the dreaded "popskull."

Gauger

The old name for a revenoo agent, as the gauger would estimate the proof and quantity of a discovered batch of likker and likewise estimate the taxes due. A definitely undesirable occupation indeed.

Grain Alcohol

Usually connoting an undiluted form of "green" spirits derived from a grain based mash.

Green Whiskey

Means first run alcohol before it is aged, filtered, or adulterated.

Groundhog Still

Refers to a still which is permanently buried in a hillside and uses the flame and heat leaving the firebox which wraps around the sides of the still. See chapter No. 3 on still building under **heating system, page 42**

Hooch

See moonshine.

Hydrometer

A thermometer-like instrument which measures the volume of alcohol in a liquid such as mash. See page

Jigger

Most often a slang term for an ounce of booze.

Makin'

Involved in the process of extracting ethanol from naturally entropic material, usually plants.

Malt

A sprouted grain, usually barley, which is dried and then ground to a granular texture which converts the insoluble starches into soluble sugar (the basis of old school moonshining). See chapter No. 4 on the Mash under **Corn** on page 52

Malted Corn

Describes corn which has been malted as mentioned in chapter No. 4 on the Mash under **the Corn** on page 52

Mash

The volume of liquid prepared by fermentation to contain a percentage of alcohol which is then distilled to produce liquor. The mash is covered in all its flaming glory in chapter No. 4, more commonly known as the Mash chapter.

Mash Box

Box constructed for the frementation of mash.

Monkey

A hired hand which loads bananas into the still. You must remember to never try to chiquita an honest man. A monkey is also a hired hand who would run the operation back when whiskey makin' was in the profitably prohibitional days.

Old School

Referring here to the method of making whiskey using sprouted grain as opposed to sugar.

Played Out Mash

Referring to sour Mash or the liquid remaining after the whiskey has been removed from the mash. See sour mash.

Popskull

A term describing the headache accompanying the defectively manufactured spirits.

Proof

Is twice the actual percentage of alcohol contained in a volume of liquid.

Proof Vial

A small clear glass bottle of approx. one ounce capacity used to determine the proof of a particular test sample.

Puke

Describes the head of the cooking mash boiling over into the connecting tubes or other parts of the still thus clouding the run.

Reruns

Doublin'.

Run

Makin', operating the still, runnin' off a batch.

Slag Box

A waystation for alcohol vapors in which they are free to dispense with excess baggage; a compartment between the still pot and the condenser coil where the impurities are trapped, and the ethanol passes on toward the condenser.

Sour Mash

The mash left in the pot after most of the alcohol has been removed from it by distilling.

Sour Mash Whiskey

Whiskey distilled from mash which is made by substituting sour mash for water.

Sprouting

To take a seed (grain) and add warm water for 24 hours, then to rinse until the grain starts to grow.

Starter

The mixture of yeast and sugar added to the rest of the ingredients in the mash to begin fermentation.

Teedum Barrel

Small aging barrel used to harbor the family stash, the cream of the still catchin's.

Thumper

Purifying device for whiskey, used in larger stills for multiple runs. An elaborate slag box.

Working

The mash as it ferments.

Worm

The copper tube in the condenser, sometimes referring to the flake box in whole.

NOTES

OLIVER PRESS BOOKS

JOSEPH ROSENBLOOM
Kits and Plans
Finder's Guide No. 1

Where to purchase plans and kits for practically anything you can think of. From mini-bikes to harpsichords, this guide tells who offers what and what it costs. *288 pages*

ISBN 0-914400-00-2   Price $3.95 paper

JOSEPH ROSENBLOOM
Craft Supplies Supermarket
Finder's Guide No. 2

An illustrated and indexed directory of craft supplies. Thousands of products including materials, kits, tools from over 450 companies are analyzed from their catalogs. *Index, illustrations, 224 pages*

ISBN 0-914400-01-0   Price $3.95 paper

ANNE HECK
The Complete Kitchen
Finder's Guide No. 3

A comprehensive guide to hard-to-find utensils. This book describes the companies supplying such utensils as well as offering information on their catalogs. *Illustrated, 96 pages*

ISBN 0-914400-02-9   Price $2.95 paper

GARY WADE
Homegrown Energy
Power for the Home and Homestead
Finder's Guide No. 4

A complete directory to the thousands of available products involved in the production of home grown power. Water wheels, solar cells, windmills and other exotic equipment are covered and indexed in depth. *Illustrated, 96 pages*

ISBN 0-914400-03-7   Price $2.95 paper

ARMAND BITEAUX
The New Consciousness
Finder's Guide No. 5

A guide to spiritual groups: name; address, international, national, local; statement of philosophy; biographies of leaders; bibliography of publications of the group. *Index, 300 pages*

ISBN 0-914400-04-5   Price $3.95 paper

ROLAND ROBERTSON
Spices, Condiments, Teas, Coffees, and Other Delicacies
Finder's Guide No. 6

This illustrated and indexed directory answers difficult questions involved with finding and purchasing unusual ingredients, beverages and foods which are difficult to obtain locally. *Index, illustrated, 208 pages*

ISBN 0-914400-05-3   Price $3.95 paper

FRED DAVIS
Country Tools
Essential Hardware and Livery
Finder's Guide No. 7

Locates sources for otherwise difficult-to-find tools essential to country living. This indispensible guide to the country resident working his land covers everything from bell scrapers to goat harnesses to spoke shavers. *Illustrated, 160 pages*

ISBN 0-914400-06-1   Price $3.95 paper

PAT FALGE and ARNOLD LEGGETT
The Complete Garden
Finder's Guide No. 8

The catalogs of over 700 garden tool and seed companies which sell by mail order organized into a comprehensive guide. From carrots to kohlrabi, from tomato stakes to rabbit repellent, it tells who sells what and how to get it. *Illustrated, 318 pages*
ISBN 0-914400-11-8   Price $3.95 paper

DERWOOD McCRAKEN
Mother Nature's Recipe Book
Mother Nature Series No. 1

Includes some 85 commonly found wild plants with detailed drawings of each plant and recipes for preparing a main course from each. Plant identification is emphasized as are tested, nutritional meals which can contribute to the average household's fight against rising food costs. *Illustrated, 160 pages*
ISBN 0-914400-07-X   Price $3.95 paper

DEZIRINA GOUZIL
Mother Nature's Herbs and Teas
Mother Nature Series No. 2

A guide to approximately 110 easily found herbs and other plants that are used in the preparation of seasonings and beverages. This introduction for the layman includes detailed illustrations of each plant and a description of its habitat. *Illustrated, 224 pages*
ISBN 0-914400-08-8   Price $3.95 paper

WILL BEARFOOT
Mother Nature's Dyes and Fibers
Mother Nature Series No. 3

A book of plants and trees utilized in the preparation of dyes and weaving materials by North American Indians. The author has drawn his research from interviews with Indians still using the original methods. Step-by-step procedures are outlined and accompanied by detailed illustrations of the plants and trees used. *Illustrated, 192 pages*
ISBN 0-914400-10-X   Price $3.95 paper

DR. JUDY WILSON
Mother Nature's Homestead First Aid
Mother Nature Series No. 4

This book is a rural emergency first aid tool, emphasizing self-help procedures for everything from sprains to major injuries. It is indispensible for those who live in remote areas with little access to professional medical help. Special attention is given to the preparation of the sick or injured for transportation to medical facilities. *Illustrated, 192 pages*
ISBN 0-914400-09-6   Price $3.95 paper

MICHAEL BARLEYCORN
Moonshiner's Manual

A do-it-yourself detailed guide to making your own whiskey. Laws of the fifty states and the Federal government are included along with chapters on history, recipes, safety and chemistry—all written in an easy to understand, delightfully entertaining manner. *Illustrated, 281 pages*
ISBN 0-914400-12-6   Price $3.95 paper

OLIVER PRESS BOOKS

Order Blank

Dear Sirs:

I believe your new **MOTHER NATURE** series fills a definite need for information and I would like to order:

QUANTITY	TITLE	TOTAL
	copies of MOTHER NATURE'S RECIPE BOOK @ $3.95 ea.	
	copies of MOTHER NATURE'S HERBS & TEAS @ $3.95 ea.	
	copies of MOTHER NATURE'S DYES & FIBERS @ $3.95 ea.	
	copies of MOTHER NATURE'S HOMESTEAD FIRST AID @ $3.95 ea.	
	copies of KITS AND PLANS @ $3.95 ea.	
	copies of CRAFT SUPPLIES SUPERMARKET @ $3.95 ea.	
	copies of THE COMPLETE KITCHEN @ $2.95 ea.	
	copies of HOMEGROWN ENERGY @ $2.95 ea.	
	copies of THE NEW CONSCIOUSNESS @ $3.95 ea.	
	copies of SPICES, CONDIMENTS, TEAS, COFFEES, AND OTHER DELICACIES @ $3.95 ea.	
	copies of COUNTRY TOOLS @ $3.95 ea.	
	copies of THE COMPLETE GARDEN @ $3.95 ea.	
	copies of MOONSHINER'S MANUAL @ $3.95 ea.	
	copies of ALL OF THE ABOVE BOOKS ($49.35 Total)	